CCORD

BASIC CARPENTRY SKILLS

ROOF
FRAMING

CHARLEY G. CHADWICK
GEORGE W. SMITH, JR.
TIM MILNER

D1736652

**American Association for
Vocational Instructional Materials**
The National Institute for Instructional Materials
745 Gaines School Road
Athens, Georgia 30605

The American Association for Vocational Instructional Materials (AAVIM) is a non-profit national institute.

The institute is a cooperative effort of universities, colleges, and divisions of vocational and technical education in the United States, established to provide excellence in instructional materials.

Direction is given by a representative from each of the member states. AAVIM also works closely with teacher organizations, government agencies and industry.

AAVIM Staff

George W. Smith, Jr.	*Interim Executive Director*
James E. Wren	*Art Director*
Karen Seabaugh	*Secretary*
Laura Ebbert	*Business Office*
Angela Paul	*Order Department*
Suzanne Gilbert	*Photocomposition*
James Anderson	*Art Staff*
Betsy A. Arrington	*Art Staff*
Dean Roberts	*Shipping Department*

Roof Framing Editorial Staff

Lois G. Harrington	*Editor*
George W. Smith, Jr.	*Associate Editor/Art Director*
Suzanne Gilbert	*Copy Editor/Typography*
Betsy A. Arrington	*Indexing/Mechanical Color Separations/Labeling*

1991

ISBN 0–89606–287–2

Authors

Charley G. Chadwick, Tim Milner, and George W. Smith, Jr. are credited with writing of this publication. Mr. Chadwick is an experienced builder and developer and is the Building Trades Teacher at Calhoun High School, Calhoun, Georgia.

Mr. Milner is a builder and serves as Building Trades Teacher at Hart County Comprehensive High School, Hartwell, Georgia.

Mr. Smith is a former illustrator, Art Director, and Production Coordinator of AAVIM. He currently serves as Interim Executive Director, AAVIM.

Reviewers

Gary M. Palmer served as reviewer of this publication. Mr. Palmer is a building contractor from Crawford, Georgia.

Contents

List of Tables

The last stage in constructing the skeleton of a dwelling is the layout, cutting, and assembly of the roof framing. The purpose of this publication is to teach the carpenter/student the skills necessary to construct the rafter roof framing for a conventional platform-framed house.

The information in this book is based on several assumptions. It is assumed that a building plan has been chosen and that the floor, walls, and ceiling have been framed as discussed and illustrated in *Floor Framing* (AAVIM, 1988), *Wall Framing* (AAVIM, 1989), and *Ceiling Framing* (AAVIM, 1990).

The functional purpose for the roof is to provide a covering for the house. It protects the structure and its occupants from rain, sun, and snow. The shape of the roof greatly influences the overall appearance of the house (Figure 1). Whatever shape is chosen from the different types that may be constructed, the main concern is to provide a roof that is functional, durable, and appealing to the eye.

Constructing roof framing is discussed under the following headings:

A. Understanding the Components of a Basic Roof Frame Assembly
B. Selecting & Estimating Materials for Roof Framing
C. Laying Out, Cutting & Installing Common Rafters for a Gable Roof
D. Framing a Gable End Overhang & Gable End
E. Laying Out, Cutting & Installing Rafters for a Hip Roof
F. Framing Dormers
G. Laying Out, Cutting & Installing Shed-type Roof Rafters
H. Estimating & Installing Roof Sheathing

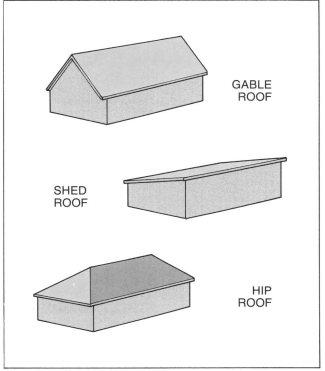

FIGURE 1. The shape of the roof has a great effect on the overall appearance of a house.

OBJECTIVES

Upon successful completion of this study unit, you will be able to do the following:

- Define terms associated with roof framing
- Identify the components of a framed roof
- Name the functions of specific roof framing members
- Select appropriate materials for construction of roof framing
- Estimate materials needed for roof framing
- Estimate the number of preassembled trusses needed for a particular job
- Name and identify the components of a roof dormer
- Lay out and install a dormer
- Lay out and install an adjoining roof assembly

A. Understanding the Components of a Basic Roof Frame Assembly

The framing of the roof assembly is the final major framing operation for the carpenter/student constructing a house. Besides having a pleasing appearance, the roof also must shed water or snow quickly. The strength of the roof must be great enough to withstand strong winds and, in some areas of the country, the weight of snow and ice, in addition to the weight of the materials used in construction.

Understanding the components of a basic roof frame assembly is discussed under the following headings:

1. Parts of a Basic Gable Roof Frame
2. Roof Pitch and Rise

1. PARTS OF A BASIC GABLE ROOF FRAME

Any discussion of roof framing involves terminology that may not be familiar to the carpenter/student. Some of the terms and components you will need to know and understand are defined below.

Bird's mouth—triangular-shaped notch cut near the bottom of a rafter that allows it to set flat on the rafter plate. The bird's mouth is made by a plumb cut and a level cut. The **crotch** of the bird's mouth is that point where the plumb cut and level cut meet.

Chord—member of a truss. The **top chord** is the rafter or sloped position. The **lower chord** is the horizontal member that acts both as a ceiling joist and as a nailing surface for ceiling materials.

Collar beam or **collar tie**—horizontal piece that ties the rafters on opposite sides of the ridgeboard together above the wall plate and in the upper third of the roof height (Figure A-1-1).

Common rafter—rafter that extends from the top of the wall plate to the ridge of a gable roof (Figure A-1-1).

Eaves or roof projection—part of the roof that extends beyond the edge of the outside wall framing.

Fascia board—horizontal board nailed to the lower trimmed ends (or tails) of rafters or to a rough fascia as a finish piece.

Fascia, fly, barge or **gable overhang rafter**—rafter that provides a frame for the overhang of the roof at the end of a gable (Figure A-1-1). This rafter is supported at the top by the ridgeboard and at the bottom by a rough fascia board (or band). Other supports are the lookouts and the roof sheathing.

Gable end—triangular-shaped area between the cap plate and the angled framing of a gable roof found at the end of a house (Figure A-1-1).

Gable roof—roof with sides that slope in opposite directions downward from the top (Figure 1).

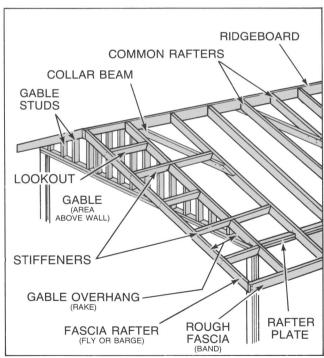

FIGURE A-1-1. Some of the components of a basic gable roof.

Gusset—plate of metal or plywood fastened and installed over two or more members of a truss to secure them together.

Hip roof—roof angle formed when two adjacent external roof slopes meet. On a hip roof, the slopes are on all four sides of the building (Figure 1).

Level cut—a cut that is a true horizontal plane (side to side) when placed in its proper position; for example, the fit between the rafter plate and the top cut of a bird's mouth (seat cut).

Lookout—framing member that projects beyond the exterior wall of a building (Figure A-1-1). Lookouts (also called **outriggers**, **ladder steps**, or **lookout braces**) may be used to help support a fascia (fly, barge) rafter on the end of a gable or to provide a nailing surface for soffit finish material, such as plywood.

Plumb cut—a cut that is a true vertical plane (up and down) when placed in proper position; for example, the cut at the top of a rafter where it joins the ridgeboard.

Purlin—board placed horizontally beneath and across roof rafters between the ridgeboard and the outside wall. It is held in place by braces that extend from the ceiling joists.

Rafter—sloping frame member of the roof that supports the sheathing, roof covering materials, and all other loads (Figure A-1-1).

Rafter plate—double plate that caps the tops of the studs that support the bottom end of the rafters (Figure A-1-1).

Rafter span—overall width of a building plus the overhang of the rafters beyond the rafter plate.

Rafter tail—part of the rafter that overhangs the rafter plate and extends from the face of the wall.

Ridgeboard or **ridge**—highest horizontal member of a roof assembly to which the top ends of rafters are attached (Figure A-1-1).

Rise—vertical distance between the rafter plate and the ridgeboard. The pitch (angle of the slope) determines the total rise.

Roof—top part of a house, consisting of a rafter frame, sheathing (roof decking), and some type of finish covering material.

Roof truss—a framework of rafters and ceiling joists with web bracing installed in a triangular arrangement using reinforcing plates (gussets) at the joints. The truss is often purchased preassembled and then lifted and secured into place on top of the rafter plates at the job site.

Run—one half of a building's span (width) when both sides of the building have an equal pitch. Two rafters, cut alike and installed on either side of a central ridgeboard, cover the total span. (If the pitch of the two sides is unequal, the rafters are longer on one side than the other, and the ridgeboard is not in the center of the roof assembly.)

Soffit—underside portion of any overhang at the ends or sides of a roof assembly.

Span—overall width of a building.

Stiffener—framing member that extends from the second common rafter, over the end rafter, out to the side of a fascia (fly, barge) rafter (Figure A-1-1). Its purpose is to give support and stability to the fascia rafter. Stiffeners are used in conjunction with lookouts to provide a nailing surface for soffit finish material.

Valley—sloped area where two roofs meet at an inside corner.

2. ROOF PITCH AND RISE

Roof *pitch* is the angle of slope of the rafters. The *total rise* of the roof is the vertical distance between (1) the top edge of the rafter plate and (2) the point where the rafter line (which runs up the rafter from the crotch of the bird's mouth) meets the middle of the ridgeboard (Figure A-2-1).

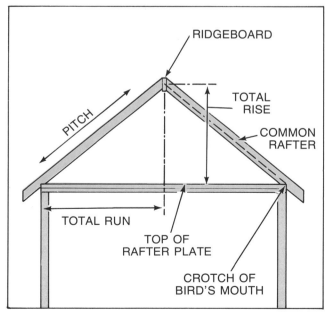

FIGURE A-2-1. Roof pitch, combined with the total run, determines the total rise.

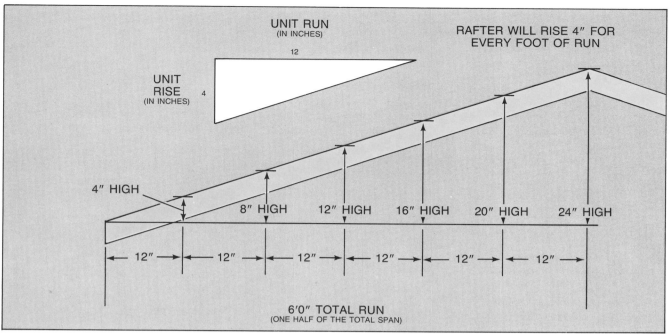

FIGURE A-2-2. The triangular symbol found on blueprints identifies the rise per foot in inches (vertically) for every foot the rafter covers (horizontally).

The total rise is calculated using information about the roof pitch and the *total run*, which is the horizontal distance between the outside of the wall and the center of the roof ridge (or half a span). Blueprints provide this information.

When you look at the blueprints for a house being built, a small triangle will be shown on the side elevation. The number to the side of the triangle gives the *unit rise* (in inches) per unit run (in inches). This means that for every foot (12″) the rafter covers horizontally (total run), the rafter will rise vertically by the number of inches shown (Figure A-2-2). The higher the unit rise number, the steeper the roof.

In order to set the roof ridge at the correct height, you must be able to use blueprint information to calculate the total rise. You do this by multiplying the number of feet in a total run by the unit rise.

As an example, calculate the total rise of a house with a 28′ span and a 6″ unit rise (Figure A-2-3). We know that a run is half a span, so first divide the total span (28′) by 2 to determine the number of feet in the total run:

$$\frac{28'}{2} = 14' \text{ total run}$$

Next, multiply the number of feet in the total run (14) by the unit rise (6″):

$$\begin{array}{r} 14 \\ \times 6'' \\ \hline 84'' \text{ total rise (in inches)} \end{array}$$

Finally, divide the total rise (84″) by 12 (number of inches in a foot) to determine the number of feet in the total rise:

$$\frac{84''}{12} = 7' \text{ total rise (in feet)}$$

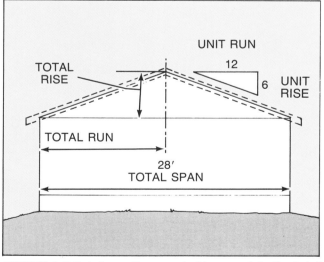

FIGURE A-2-3. Information needed to calculate the total rise of a roof: 28′ wide (span) with a 6″ unit rise.

STUDY QUESTIONS

Part 1: Matching

The list on the left contains the names of key roof framing components. The list on the right provides statements that describe the nature and/or function of various roof components. Select the statement that most accurately describes each component, and place the letter of that response in the blank to the left of that component. **NOTE:** There are more responses than components listed, so you will have some responses left over.

_____ 1. Hip roof

_____ 2. Gable roof

_____ 3. Ridgeboard

_____ 4. Common rafter

_____ 5. Fascia rafter

_____ 6. Lookout

_____ 7. Collar beam

_____ 8. Fascia board

_____ 9. Bird's mouth

_____ 10. Level cut

_____ 11. Plumb cut

_____ 12. Span

_____ 13. Rise

_____ 14. Run

_____ 15. Pitch

a. Cut that is a true horizontal plane when placed in its proper position

b. Angle of slope of the rafters

c. Member of a truss

d. Half the building's width when both sides of the building have an equal pitch

e. Triangular-shaped notch cut in a rafter so that it sets flat on the rafter plate

f. Roof with slopes on all four sides of the building

g. Vertical distance between the rafter plate and the ridgeboard

h. Double plate that supports the bottom ends of the rafters

i. Part of "ladder steps" that project beyond the exterior wall of the building

j. Horizontal piece that ties rafters together above the wall plate

k. Roof with sides that slope in opposite directions down from the top

l. Cut that is a true vertical plane when placed in its proper position

m. Roof component that runs down from the ridgeboard and provides a frame for the overhang of the roof at the end of a gable

n. Overall width of a building

o. Highest horizontal member of a roof assembly to which the top ends of rafters are attached

p. Horizontal piece nailed to rafter tails as a finish piece

q. Roof component that extends from the top of the wall plate to the ridge of a gable roof

Part II: Calculations

1. Calculate the total rise (in feet) when the total span is 40' and the unit rise is 3".

2. Calculate the total rise (in feet) when the total run is 18' and the unit rise is 5".

B. Selecting & Estimating Materials for Roof Framing

A number of factors must be considered in selecting materials for roof framing; for example:

- Local code requirements
- Architect's design
- Specifications
- Price
- Availability of materials
- Span
- Load
- On-center spacing
- Size of lumber
- Species of lumber

These factors are discussed in other publications in the basic carpentry series: *Floor Framing* (AAVIM, 1988), *Wall Framing* (AAVIM, 1989), and *Ceiling Framing* (AAVIM, 1990). You may wish to review the discussion in these books before proceeding.

Selecting and estimating materials for roof framing is discussed under the following headings:

1. Types and Grades of Lumber Used in Roof Framing
2. Measuring and Figuring Lumber
3. Determining the Length of a Common Rafter
4. Estimating Rafter Material for a Gable Roof Assembly
5. Estimating Material for the Gable End
6. Nails and Brackets Used in Roof Framing

1. TYPES AND GRADES OF LUMBER USED IN ROOF FRAMING

Southern pine and western white woods such as spruce, pine, fir, and hemlock are most commonly used in roof framing.

Conventionally framed roof rafters (also known as stick built) are generally made from 2" x 6" or 2" x 8" lumber, although some larger material is used where the span is larger.

Structural softwood used for roof rafter framing is classified as **dimension lumber**. Dimension lumber is also known as framing and structural joists and planks. It is at least 2" thick (nominal) and is 5" wide (nominal) and wider.[1]

In addition to rafter material, various other components of the roof framing (e.g., collar beams or ties) will require lumber of different sizes. The gable ends of the structure, for example, will be framed with 2" x 4" lumber.

Table I provides information that can help you in making correct decisions about the size and species of lumber to purchase. The straightness and structural strength of a roof frame will be determined in large part by these decisions—by the quality of the rafters and their spacing. Most builders prefer to use No. 2 grade lumber, and no lumber lower than No. 3 grade should ever be used. All lumber should be kiln-dried and grade stamped.

Lumber grades are based on the quality of the wood. Many factors, such as strength, appearance, and moisture content, affect the grade. The lower grades will have splits, separations (checks), warpage, and loose knots. The higher the grade, the fewer the defects to be found.

---

1. This information adapted from *Grading Rules*, Section 113, Size Classifications, Southern Pine Inspection Bureau (Pensacola, Florida, 1977).

Table I

Allowable Spans—High Slope Rafters
Slope Greater Than 3 in 12
(Light Roof Covering)

Liveload 20 lb./sq. ft.
Deadload 7 lb./sq. ft.
Deflection—1/180th of span
7 Day Loading

Spans Are Based on Repetitive Member

Size in Inches	Spacing in Inches	Maximum Allowable Spans in Feet and Inches										
		Southern Pine					Douglas Fir-Larch		Hem-Fir		Spruce-Pine-Fir	
		No. 1 KD*	No. 1 SD	No. 2 KD*	No. 2 SD	No. 3 SD	No. 2	No. 3	No. 2	No. 3	No. 2	No. 3
2 × 6	12	17-8	17-4	17-0	17-0	13-8	17-4	14-1	16-3	12-6	15-3	11-7
	16	16-1	15-9	15-6	15-6	11-10	15-9	12-2	14-2	10-10	13-2	10-0
	24	14-1	13-9	13-3	12-9	9-8	13-0	9-11	11-7	8-10	10-9	8-2
2 × 8	12	23-4	22-10	22-5	22-5	18-0	22-10	18-6	21-5	16-6	20-1	15-3
	16	21-2	20-9	20-5	20-5	15-7	20-9	16-1	18-9	14-4	17-5	13-3
	24	18-6	18-2	17-6	16-10	12-9	17-1	13-1	15-3	11-8	14-2	10-10
2 × 10	12	29-9	29-2	28-7	28-7	23-0	29-2	23-8	27-5	21-1	25-8	19-6
	16	27-1	26-6	26-0	26-0	19-11	26-6	20-6	23-11	18-3	22-3	16-11
	24	23-8	23-2	22-3	21-6	16-3	21-10	16-8	19-6	14-11	18-2	13-9
2 × 12	12	36-2	35-6	34-10	34-10	27-11	35-6	28-9	33-4	25-7	31-3	23-9
	16	32-11	32-3	31-8	31-8	24-2	32-3	24-10	29-1	22-2	27-0	20-6
	24	28-9	28-2	27-1	26-2	19-9	26-7	20-3	23-9	18-1	22-1	16-9

*KD—(Surfaced at 15 percent maximum moisture content-KD)

When purchasing lumber for rafters, pay special attention to the grade stamp found on each piece. Much valuable information about the uses and expected performance of a particular piece of lumber can be obtained from an understanding of these markings.

One of the more important things to look for in grade-marking information concerns the moisture content. The drier the wood, the more stable it will be. Wood with a moisture content over 19 percent is more likely to warp or shrink as it dries out.

Sample grade stamps for western and southern softwoods and short explanations of the marks and symbols are shown in Figure B-1-1.

For more information about lumber and grading, contact the *National Forest Products Association*, 1250 Connecticut Avenue, N.W., Washington, D.C. 20036; *Southern Forest Products Association*, P.O. Box 52468, New Orleans, Louisiana 70152; and *Western Wood Products Association*, Yeon Building, 522 S.W. Fifth Avenue, Portland, Oregon 97204.

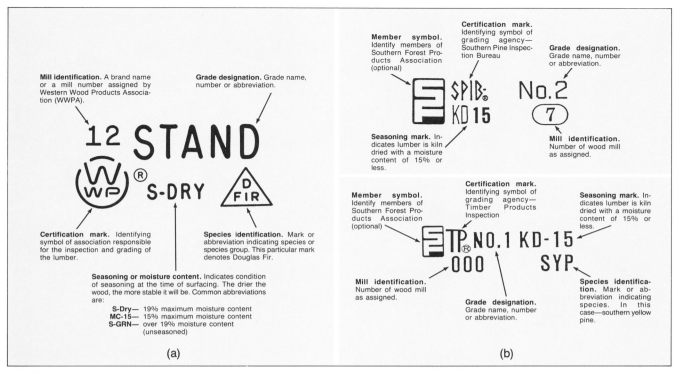

FIGURE B-1-1. Typical grade stamps and information found on (a) western wood and (b) southern pine lumber (two different marks).

2. MEASURING AND FIGURING LUMBER

When you order lumber for roof framing, you will need to know the quantity, size, and length of the pieces.

Lumber dimensions are referred to by *nominal dimensions*, which are different from *actual dimensions.* This difference is due to the changes that take place in a piece of lumber in the manufacturing process. A piece of lumber is cut from a tree, cut to a rough size (**nominal dimensions**), and then subjected to drying and surfacing that reduce the material to its **actual** size.

A comparison and more detailed discussion of nominal- and actual-sized lumber can be found in *Floor Framing* (AAVIM, 1988).

When ordering lumber, remember the following guidelines:

- Measurements are always given in the following order: thickness, width, and length (Figure B-2-1).

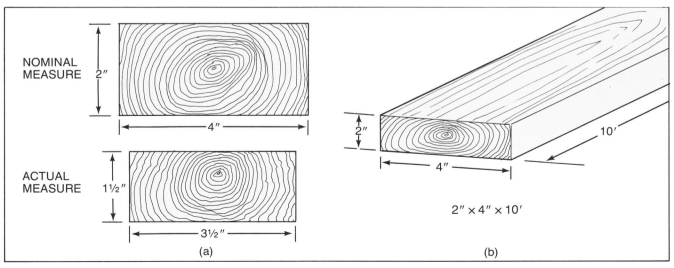

FIGURE B-2-1. (a) The nominal and actual dimensions of lumber are different. (b) Lumber measurements are always given in the following order: thickness, width, and length.

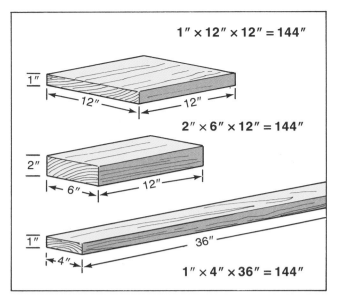

FIGURE B-2-2. A board foot is a unit of quantity for lumber equal to any piece of lumber with a volume of 144 cubic inches.

- Lumber is sold by the *board foot*. A board foot is a unit of quantity for lumber equal to any piece of lumber 1″ × 12″ × 12″ or any other measurement with a volume of *144 cubic inches* (Figure B-2-2).

To find out how many board feet there are in a particular piece of lumber, use the following formula. Remember "**T**" = thickness (in inches), "**W**" = width (in inches), and "**L**" = length (in feet). You do not need to convert feet to inches before multiplying.

Formula	Example
$\dfrac{T \times W \times L}{12}$ = board feet	$\dfrac{2″ \times 6″ \times 14′}{12}$ = 14 board feet

When constructing a roof frame, many pieces of lumber of the same size will be ordered. If, for example, the roof you are constructing will utilize ninety 2″ × 6″ × 14′ pieces of lumber, use the following formula:

$$\frac{\text{Number of pieces} \times T \times W \times L}{12}$$

$$\frac{90 \times 2 \times 6 \times 14}{12} = 1260 \text{ board feet}$$

To determine the cost for this lumber, multiply the number of board feet (1260) by the cost per board foot (assume a cost of $500 per thousand B.F., or 50¢ per foot):

```
    1260
  × .50
  ──────
    0000
    6300
  ──────
```
$630.00 total cost for 1260 board feet

You may wish to make up a bill of materials form on which you record this valuable information (Figure B-2-3). A blank form is provided on page 94.

- Although the actual *thickness* and *width* are smaller, you request lumber by its nominal measurements. Lumber is always figured based on nominal measurements (Figure B-2-1).
- The *length* of all lumber (except precut studs) will always be the actual length. For example, a piece of lumber 2″ thick (nominal) by 6″ wide (nominal) by 14′ long (actual) will actually measure 1½″ × 5½″ × 14′ (or slightly over) but will be called a 2″ × 6″ × 14′.
- Lumber is generally sold in even foot lengths ranging from 8′ to 16′, with longer pieces available (on order) at an increased cost.

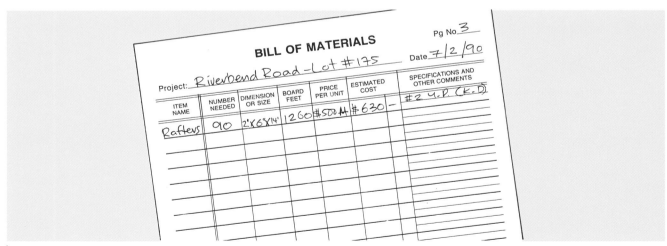

FIGURE B-2-3. A portion of a bill of materials form with information recorded on some of the roof framing materials needed.

14

Prices vary on lumber so it is wise to check with several suppliers before buying. Other variables, such as grade, length, and species, have an effect on price.

Some building supply stores price lumber by the piece rather than by the board foot. If this is the case, determine the number of pieces needed of a particular size and length. Using the previous example, assume the roof framing requires ninety 2″ × 6″ × 14′ pieces. Assume the price per piece is $7.00. To determine the total cost, multiply the cost per piece by the number of pieces needed:

$$\begin{array}{r} \$\ \ 7.00 \\ \underline{\times\,90} \\ \$630.00 \ \ \text{total cost} \end{array}$$

Again, record this information on your bill of materials form.

To find the cost per board foot of an individual piece, first use the formula T × W × L ÷ 12 to determine the number of board feet. For example:

$$\frac{2 \times 6 \times 14}{12} = 14 \text{ B.F.}$$

Take the number of board feet in this piece (14) and divide it into the cost per piece ($7.00):

$$\frac{\$7.00}{14} = \begin{array}{l} 50\text{¢ per B.F. or} \\ \$500 \text{ per thousand B.F.} \end{array}$$

3. DETERMINING THE LENGTH OF A COMMON RAFTER

In order to estimate the amount of lumber needed for a gable roof frame, you must first find the length of an individual rafter. The length of a rafter is based on the unit rise and total run of the roof. These values can be found by examining the blueprints of the house you are building, as discussed in Section A-2.

Many carpenters prefer to use a book of rafter tables, which contain rafter measurements for a wide range of roof spans and unit rises. There are other methods, but our discussion will focus on using a steel framing square with a stamped rafter table (Figure B-3-1). Other rafter tables, which provide the length of rafters for several commonly used roof pitches, are included in the appendix for those who wish to use them. Your instructor can help you with the procedures necessary to use the tables correctly.

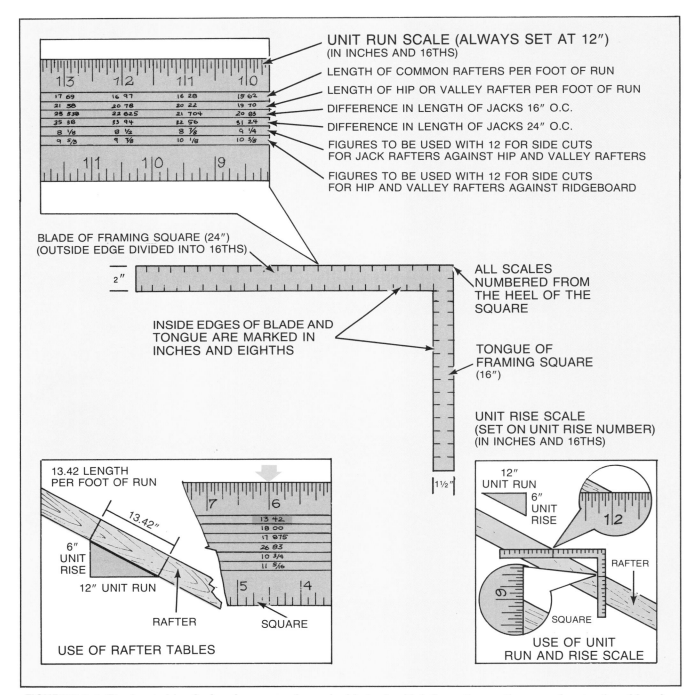

UNIT RUN SCALE (ALWAYS SET AT 12″)
(IN INCHES AND 16THS)

LENGTH OF COMMON RAFTERS PER FOOT OF RUN

LENGTH OF HIP OR VALLEY RAFTER PER FOOT OF RUN

DIFFERENCE IN LENGTH OF JACKS 16″ O.C.

DIFFERENCE IN LENGTH OF JACKS 24″ O.C.

FIGURES TO BE USED WITH 12 FOR SIDE CUTS FOR JACK RAFTERS AGAINST HIP AND VALLEY RAFTERS

FIGURES TO BE USED WITH 12 FOR SIDE CUTS FOR HIP AND VALLEY RAFTERS AGAINST RIDGEBOARD

BLADE OF FRAMING SQUARE (24″)
(OUTSIDE EDGE DIVIDED INTO 16THS)

2″

INSIDE EDGES OF BLADE AND TONGUE ARE MARKED IN INCHES AND EIGHTHS

ALL SCALES NUMBERED FROM THE HEEL OF THE SQUARE

TONGUE OF FRAMING SQUARE (16″)

UNIT RISE SCALE (SET ON UNIT RISE NUMBER)
(IN INCHES AND 16THS)

1½″

13.42 LENGTH PER FOOT OF RUN

13.42″

6″ UNIT RISE

12″ UNIT RUN

RAFTER

SQUARE

USE OF RAFTER TABLES

12″ UNIT RUN

6″ UNIT RISE

RAFTER

SQUARE

USE OF UNIT RUN AND RISE SCALE

FIGURE B-3-1. The front side of a framing square is a valuable tool, with information on the many facets of roof framing.

A **steel framing square** is an L-shaped, flat metal tool with one 24″ leg called the **blade** and one 16″ leg called the **tongue**. The framing square is designed for use in laying out angles and calculating lengths of framing members. Most are etched with tables commonly used in carpentry calculations.

To assist you in using a framing square, you may wish to purchase and use a small accessory called a **stair gauge clamp**. This device is fastened to the edge of the framing square at the proper pitch line. This keeps the framing square in a fixed position. Thus, accuracy and speed of layout are greatly increased, since

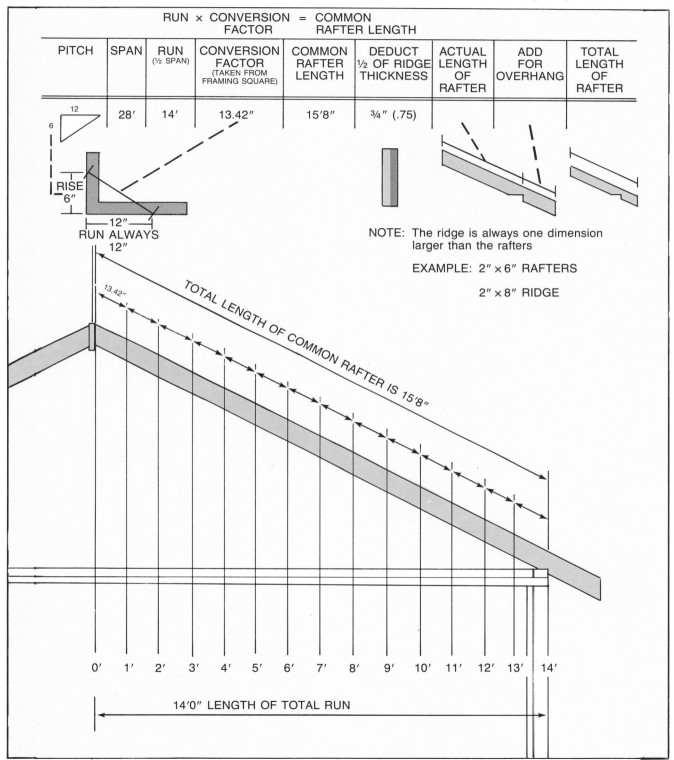

PITCH	SPAN	RUN (½ SPAN)	CONVERSION FACTOR (TAKEN FROM FRAMING SQUARE)	COMMON RAFTER LENGTH	DEDUCT ½ OF RIDGE THICKNESS	ACTUAL LENGTH OF RAFTER	ADD FOR OVERHANG	TOTAL LENGTH OF RAFTER
	28′	14′	13.42″	15′8″	¾″ (.75)			

RUN × CONVERSION FACTOR = COMMON RAFTER LENGTH

NOTE: The ridge is always one dimension larger than the rafters

EXAMPLE: 2″ × 6″ RAFTERS

2″ × 8″ RIDGE

FIGURE B-3-2. A chart (top) may help you to organize the information gathered using a framing square. The roof in question is diagrammed in the bottom section of this illustration.

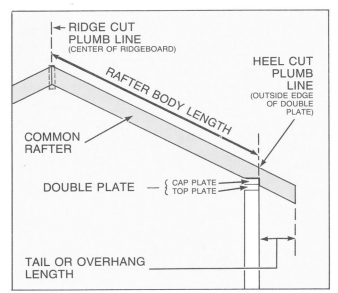

FIGURE B-3-3. The body length of a rafter is measured from the ridge plumb cut line to the heel plumb cut line.

checking marks on the square (a time-consuming task) is not necessary.

You can figure rafter lengths using the side of the framing square used for rafter work (called the **rafter tables**). As an example, determine the length of a common rafter for a house with a 6″ unit rise and a total run of 14′. You will need an actual framing square for this exercise. If you don't have one, see your instructor. You may also wish to use a chart to help you organize your calculations (Figure B-3-2). Proceed as follows:

1. *Look at the blade (the 24″ long leg) of the framing square, and find the line reading "length common rafters per foot run."*

2. *Locate the number at the top of the blade that represents the unit rise (6″).*

3. *Look directly below the unit rise number (6), and read the number on the first line.*

   You will find this number to be 13.42. This means that a common rafter with a 6″ unit rise will be 13.42″ long for each foot of run.

4. *Multiply the length of common rafter per foot of run (13.42″) by the number of feet in the total run (14). Remember the total run is always half the width of the total span.*

$$\begin{array}{r} 13.42'' \\ \times\ 14 \\ \hline 5368 \\ 1342 \\ \hline 187.88'' \end{array}$$

5. *Change the decimal (.88″) to a fraction by multiplying by 16 (because inches are divided into 16ths).*

$$\begin{array}{r} .88 \\ \times 16 \\ \hline 528 \\ 88 \\ \hline 14.08 \end{array}$$

The number to the left of the decimal point (14) is the number of 16ths in the fraction; in our example, this is $^{14}/_{16}$″. The number to the right of the decimal represents tenths (one place) or hundredths (two places) of $^{1}/_{16}$″; in our example, this is $^{08}/_{100}$.

Since $^{08}/_{100}$ is so small, it is not figured in the final equation. If the number to the right of the decimal point amounts to $^{50}/_{100}$ (or more) of $^{1}/_{16}$″, add $^{1}/_{16}$″ to the figure on the left side of the decimal point (rounded off).

Finally, reduce $^{14}/_{16}$″ to its lowest common denominator. In this case, 14 and 16 can both be divided by 2:

$$\frac{14''}{16} = \frac{7''}{8}$$

Thus, the length of each rafter in inches is 187.88″ or 187$^{7}/_{8}$″.

6. *Convert the total inches into feet and inches. (Use Table II to convert $^{7}/_{8}$″ to a decimal equivalent.) To convert, take the total number of whole inches (187), add the decimal equivalent for the fraction ($^{7}/_{8}$ = .8750), and divide by 12 (the number of inches in a foot).*

$$\frac{187.8750''}{12} = 15.65625'$$

The number to the left of the decimal point is the length in **whole feet** of the rafter in our example (15′). The number to the right of the decimal point (.65625) is a decimal fraction of a foot; it must be converted to inches. This is done by multiplying the decimal fraction by 12 (the number of inches in a foot):

$$\begin{array}{r} .65625 \\ \times\ 12 \\ \hline 131250 \\ 65625 \\ \hline 7.87500'' \end{array}$$

The answer (7.875″) should be rounded to the next highest whole number (8″). Thus, the common body rafter in our example should have a length of 15.65625′ or 15′8″.

The determined body length of the rafter (Figure B-3-3) measures from the **ridge plumb cut line** (the center of the ridgeboard) to the **heel plumb cut line** (the outside edge of the double plate).

Table II
Decimal Equivalents

Fraction	Decimal Equivalent	Fraction	Decimal Equivalent
1/16	.0625	9/16	.5625
1/8	.1250	5/8	.6250
3/16	.1875	11/16	.6875
1/4	.2500	3/4	.7500
5/16	.3125	13/16	.8125
3/8	.3750	7/8	.8750
7/16	.4375	15/16	.9375
1/2	.5000	1	1.000

NOTE: To change a fraction to a decimal fraction, divide the numerator by the denominator. For example, 1/16 = 1 ÷ 16 = .0625.

7. *Add the tail or overhang length to the measurement. The tail or overhang length is the distance beyond the frame wall* (Figure B-3-3).

If the length of the rafter is 15′8″ from the ridge plumb cut line to the heel plumb cut line and you want a 12″ (or 1′) overhang, the two figures must be added to determine the total length of materials needed:

```
  15′8″
 + 1′0″
  16′8″   total length needed
```

Since lumber is sold by the foot in even-numbered increments and the rafter in our example has to be at least 16′8″ long, it would be wise to purchase rafter material 18′0″ to allow for any end splits or damaged lumber ends.

The rafter will also have to be *shortened* at the ridge cut end by one half the thickness of the ridgeboard. Since most ridgeboards are 1½″ thick, the rafter length will have to be shortened ¾″. This adjustment will be discussed further in the step-by-step procedures in Section C.

4. ESTIMATING RAFTER MATERIAL FOR A GABLE ROOF ASSEMBLY

Once the length of lumber needed for rafters has been determined, you need to calculate the number of rafters needed. Rafters are normally placed 16″ O.C. (on-center) or 24″ O.C.

To estimate the number of rafters needed, proceed as follows:

1. *Determine the linear feet of the front wall of the house* (Figure B-4-1).

The floor plan of the house has a 60′ front wall.

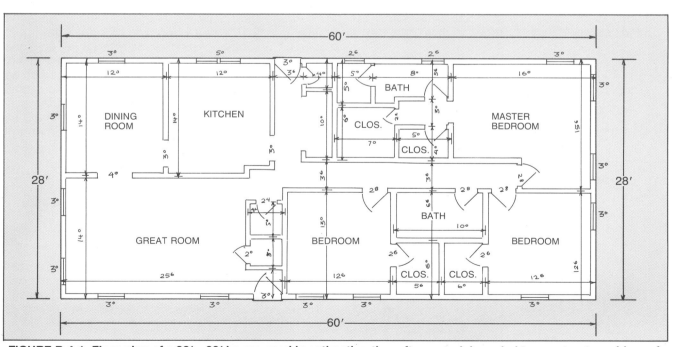

FIGURE B-4-1. Floor plan of a 28′ × 60′ house used in estimating the rafter material needed to construct a gable roof.

19

2. *Divide the linear feet by the rafter spacing.*

If your rafter spacing is 16″ O.C., take ¾ of the linear front wall measurement (i.e., multiply linear front wall measurement by .75). In the event you are using 24″ O.C. spacing, divide the linear front wall measurement by 2. Given 60 linear feet of front wall and 16″ O.C. rafter spacing:

$$
\begin{array}{r}
60' \\
\times\,.75 \\
\hline
300 \\
420 \\
\hline
45.00 \text{ rafters}
\end{array}
$$

(round number up or down to the nearest whole number if needed)

3. *Add two rafters for each end rafter and two more for the gable overhangs.*

$$
\begin{array}{rl}
45 & \text{rafters} \\
2 & \text{end rafters} \\
2 & \text{gable overhang rafters} \\
\hline
49 & \text{rafters needed for front side}
\end{array}
$$

NOTE: The number of rafters may also be affected by the addition of dormers to the roof. This will be discussed in Section F.

4. *Double the number to determine the total rafters needed for the front and back sides of the house.*

$$
\begin{array}{rl}
49 & \\
\times\,2 & \\
\hline
98 & \text{rafters needed for front} \\
 & \text{and back sides of house}
\end{array}
$$

Material for a ridgeboard must also be figured (Figure B-4-2). Remember the ridgeboard is the horizontal member at the top of the gable roof assembly. It is located between the ridge plumb cut ends of the rafters.

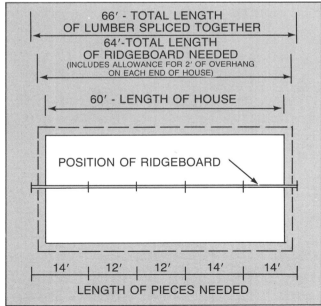

FIGURE B-4-2. A simple diagram can help you visualize the factors to be considered when estimating the ridgeboard.

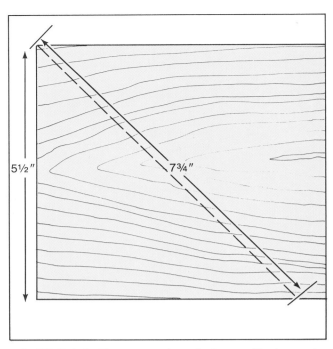

FIGURE B-4-3. The top end angled cut will always be longer than the width of the board, regardless of the angle being cut. In this example, a 6″ (nominal) board has an angled cut measuring 7¾″.

Ridgeboard lumber should be one dimension size wider than that used for rafters. For example, if your rafters are made from 2″ × 6″ material, use 2″ × 8″ lumber for the ridgeboard. This is because the ends of rafters are cut at an angle. Thus, the top end cut is longer than the width of the rafter material (Figure B-4-3).

The ridgeboard need not be figured exactly, since the ends can be trimmed when the end rafters are put in place. The ridgeboard will normally be longer than one piece of lumber. Therefore, it will have to be spliced. A diagram of the house, roof, and the projected overhang (Figure B-4-2) shows that three 14′ pieces and two 12′ pieces will span the length and the projected overhang. A 1′ margin should be provided on either end and should then be trimmed off when the rafters are nailed in place.

Add all these figures to your material list.

Material	Purpose	Estimated Number Needed
2″ × 6″ × 18′	rafters	98
2″ × 8″ × 14′	ridgeboard	3
2″ × 8″ × 12′	ridgeboard	2

NOTE: Four 2″ × 8″ × 16′ pieces could instead be used for the ridgeboard. A total of 64′ of lumber is needed for the ridgeboard, with little allowance for waste. Therefore, four 16′ pieces would be sufficient if no ends were trimmed.

5. ESTIMATING MATERIAL FOR THE GABLE END

Material for framing the triangular area between the rafter framing and the top of the end wall frame must also be figured. This triangular area is called the **gable end**.

To determine the amount of lumber needed, you must first estimate the length of the studs in the gable end. These studs, called **gable studs**, decrease in length from the peak or ridge of the roof toward the outside wall (Figure B-5-1).

Although the studs in one half of a gable end are all of different lengths, the difference in overall length between adjacent studs is the same. This constant distance, known as the *common length difference*, is found on the information on the framing square.

The method described here utilizes the framing square to determine the length of gable studs for a house with a $^6/_{12}$ pitch a span of 28', and 16" O.C. spacing between gable studs. In Section A-2, the total rise of such a structure was determined to be 7'0". Therefore, if the gable is being framed with the first stud under the ridgeboard, it can be assumed that the first stud is 7'0" long, with others (toward the outside wall) being progressively shorter.

To estimate material for the gable end, proceed as follows:

1. *Position the framing square across a piece of lumber with the blade leg to your left and the tongue to your right.*

2. *Move the square until the 12" mark on the blade leg is even with the top edge of the board and the 6"*

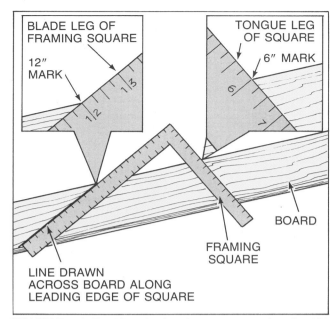

FIGURE B-5-2. Position the framing square so that the 12" mark on the blade and the 6" mark (unit rise) on the tongue are even with the edge of the board. Draw a line along the leading edge of the blade.

mark on the tongue leg is also even with the top of the board (Figure B-5-2).

The 12" mark is used because the unit run is figured in feet (12"). The 6" mark on the tongue is used since the unit rise is 6" per foot of run.

3. *Draw a line across the lumber along the leading edge of the blade* (Figure B-5-2).

4. *Slide the framing square blade upward along the line you've just drawn until the 16" mark is at the edge of the lumber* (Figure B-5-3).

The 16" mark is used because the on-center spacing of the gable studs is 16".

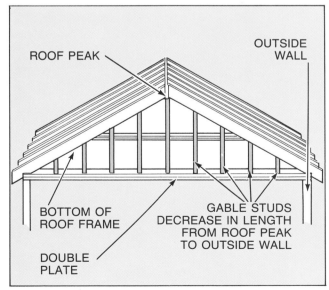

FIGURE B-5-1. The gable studs fit in the triangular area between the top of the double plate and the bottom of the roof frame.

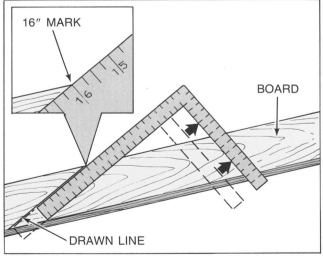

FIGURE B-5-3. Move the framing square upward along the line previously drawn until the 16" mark (O.C. spacing) is at the edge of the lumber.

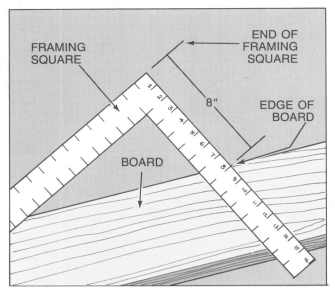

FIGURE B-5-4. The distance between the end of the framing square and the edge of the board is the common length difference for gable studs.

5. *Identify the distance in inches from the top end of the framing square to the place where the tongue crosses the edge of the board* (Figure B-5-4).

The figure you find (in this case, 8″) is the common length difference for the gable studs. Each successive gable stud will be shorter than the adjacent stud by 8″.

NOTE: The common length difference will always be 1.33 of the unit rise when the studs are placed 16″ O.C.:

$$\begin{array}{r} 1.33 \\ \times \ 6'' \ \text{unit rise} \\ \hline 7.98'', \text{rounded to } 8'' \end{array}$$

Before the overall length of each stud can be measured, you must first determine how many gable studs there will be in half of the gable end. Proceed as follows:

1. *Multiply the number of feet in the total run (14) by 12 (number of inches in a foot).*

$$\begin{array}{r} 14 \\ \times 12 \\ \hline 28 \\ 14 \\ \hline 168 \ \text{inches in total run} \end{array}$$

2. *Divide the inches in the total run (168) by the distance between the gable studs (16″) to determine the number of studs in half of one gable end.*

$$\frac{168}{16} = 10.5 \ \text{studs needed}$$

NOTE: The .5 stud may be so short as not to be figured into the materials needed. As this example will work out, this stud would only be 4″ long.

3. *Draw a simple diagram of half the gable end to help you determine the placement of the gable studs (Figure B-5-5).*

Draw in the central stud and indicate that it is 7′0″ long (already determined). Then draw additional studs in your diagram and indicate the length of each. The length of each can be determined by subtracting 8″ (the common length difference) from the length of the adjacent stud.

This sketch will identify the length of the last two shorter studs on each half. Do not include lumber for these shorter studs in your materials list. Scrap lumber should be available around the job site to meet these needs.

4. *Use your diagram to determine the number and lengths of 2″ × 4″ lumber pieces needed to frame both gable ends, and make a chart listing the lengths of pieces needed, the number needed, and the lengths of lumber required to minimize waste.*

Two central studs and four studs of each of the other lengths will be required to frame both gable ends. Since lumber is sold in even-foot lengths, some waste will be encountered. You need to figure closely to minimize waste and avoid extra cost, as shown on the chart below.

Stud length	Number needed	Length needed to minimize waste	Number of studs cut from each piece	Number pieces to buy
7′0″	2	14′	2	1
6′4″	4	14′	2	2
5′8″	4	12′	2	2
5′0″	4	10′	2	2
4′4″	4	10′	2	2
3′8″	4	16′	4	1
3′0″	4	12′	4	1
2′4″	4	10′	4	1

5. *Add the figures to your materials list.*

Material	Purpose	Estimated Number Needed
2″ × 4″ × 16′	gable end studs	1
2″ × 4″ × 14′	gable end studs	3
2″ × 4″ × 12′	gable end studs	3
2″ × 4″ × 10′	gable end studs	5

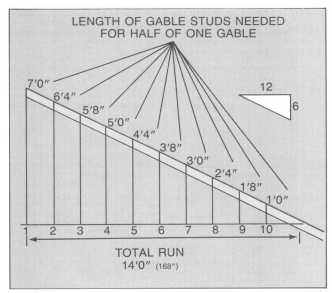

FIGURE B-5-5. A diagram can help in determining the placement of the gable studs and their lengths.

There is another way to estimate the material for the gable ends, which is faster but increases the likelihood of waste. Proceed as follows:

1. *Total the linear feet needed for all gable studs (both ends).*

   First, multiply the length of the pieces needed by the number of pieces needed. Then, add up the totals. For example:

   $$
   \begin{array}{rcl}
   1 \times 14 &=& 14 \\
   2 \times 14 &=& 28 \\
   2 \times 12 &=& 24 \\
   2 \times 10 &=& 20 \\
   2 \times 10 &=& 20 \\
   1 \times 16 &=& 16 \\
   1 \times 12 &=& 12 \\
   1 \times 12 &=& 12 \\
   \hline
   && 146 \text{ linear feet}
   \end{array}
   $$

2. *Divide the total by 14' (a long piece of lumber easily obtainable).*

   $$\frac{146}{14} = 10.4 \text{ pieces 14' in length, rounded to 10}$$

3. *Add one more 14' piece to your total.*

   This extra piece takes care of the partial (.4) piece that the calculations indicate is needed and provides extra lumber for any other short pieces required.

   $$
   \begin{array}{r}
   10 \\
   +\,1 \\
   \hline
   11 \text{ pieces 14' in length}
   \end{array}
   $$

4. *Record the total on your materials list.*

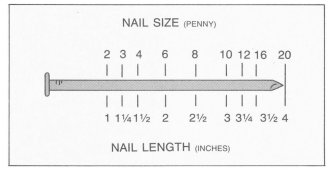

FIGURE B-6-1. A comparison between so-called "penny" sizes of nails and their actual length in inches. As the size (d number) increases, the wire gauge (diameter) also increases.

6. NAILS AND BRACKETS USED IN ROOF FRAMING

The most popular and most widely used metal fastening device in all phases of roof framing is the **coated common nail**.

Although nails are made of several metals and use different coatings, the cement-coated wire nail is the most widely used. It is cut from wire, given a head and a point, and then coated with an adhesive to provide increased holding power.

Common wire nails are available in sizes ranging from 2d (1″ long) to 60d (6″ long). See Figure B-6-1 for an example and sizes. Nail sizes are designated by a number and the letter **d**. The letter stands for **denarius**—the Roman word for coin or penny, coming from the time in England when nails were purchased according to how many pennies they cost per hundred. Larger nails cost more per hundred than do smaller sizes.

Today, nails are sold by the pound. Builders generally buy the nails used in roof framing by the 50 lb. box. A comparison of the number of nails of different sizes per pound can be seen in Table III. Most roof framing will involve the use of 10d and 16d nails; 8d nails are used in securing plywood or other sheathing material to the rafters.

Table III
Nails Used in Roof Framing

Size	Length (in)	Diameter	Number per pound
8d	2½	.131	106
10d	3	.148	69
12d	3¼	.148	63
16d	3½	.165	49

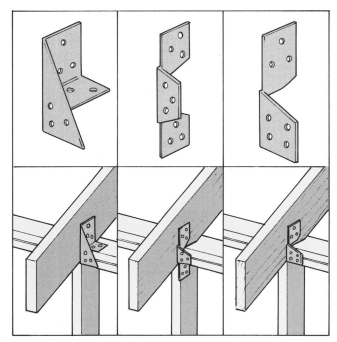

FIGURE B-6-2. Various metal rafter brackets (or anchors or hurricane tie downs) are used to secure the bottom of rafters to the double plate (top plate and cap plate).

Metal rafter brackets (or **anchors** or **hurricane tie downs**) are used to secure rafters to double plates or the supporting wall. There are many configurations of these stamp-formed devices, but all are designed to be nailed to the rafter and to a supporting member (plate) below (Figure B-6-2).

STUDY QUESTIONS

1. Name one example of a western white wood.

2. What **two** sizes of lumber are typically used for conventionally framed roof rafters?

3. What is the lowest grade of lumber that should be used for roof framing?

4. What is an acceptable moisture content level for wood?

5. When ordering lumber, which measurement is always given first?

6. When a piece of lumber is described as a 2″ × 4″, is that its actual or nominal measurements?

7. In what range of lengths is lumber commonly sold?

8. What is the volume of a board foot?

9. What is the formula for calculating board feet?

10. The length of a rafter is calculated based on what **two** values?

11. What is the length of the framing square blade?

12. The 16″ leg of a framing square is called what?

13. Where on the framing square blade do you look to find the length of common rafters per foot of run?

14. The determined body length of a rafter is measured from the ridge plumb cut line to what other line?

15. By how much should the rafter length be extended to allow for the tail or overhang?

16. The rafter length should be shortened by half the thickness of what roof component?

17. If the front wall measures 70′ and rafters will be spaced 24″ O.C., how many rafters (total) will be needed for the front and back sides of the house?

18. What dimension size should ridgeboard lumber be in comparison to the rafters?

19. In estimating the common length difference for gable studs, assume that you first position the square so that the 4″ mark on the tongue and the 12″ mark on the blade are even with the top of a board. After drawing a line across the leading edge, you move the blade up along that line until the 24″ mark is at the edge of the lumber.

    a. What does the 4″ mark represent?

    b. What does the 12″ mark represent?

    c. What does the 24″ mark represent?

20. A quick way to calculate the common length difference for gable studs placed 16″ O.C. is to multiply the unit rise by what number?

21. To calculate the number of gable studs in half a gable end, you divide the total run (in inches) by what value?

22. What **two** nail sizes are most commonly used in roof framing?

C.   Laying Out, Cutting & Installing Common Rafters for a Gable Roof

After selecting materials, estimating their cost, and ordering lumber, you are ready to lay out, cut, and install common rafters.

Laying out, cutting, and installing common rafters is discussed under the following headings:

1. Marking Rafter Locations on the Cap Plate
2. Laying Out and Cutting a Common Rafter
3. Testing Rafters for Fit
4. Splicing and Marking a Ridgeboard
5. Erecting a Gable Roof Frame
6. Installing Collar Beams (or Ties)
7. Installing Braces to Help Support Rafters

1. MARKING RAFTER LOCATIONS ON THE CAP PLATE

The proposed location of the rafters should be marked at the time the ceiling joists are laid out. Rafter layout

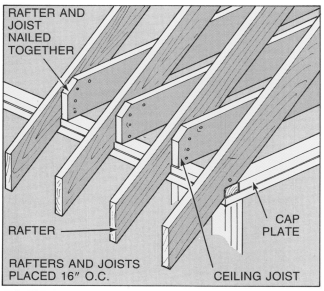

FIGURE C-1-1. Rafters spaced 16″ O.C. and nailed to the sides of ceiling joists spaced 16″ O.C. and already nailed in position.

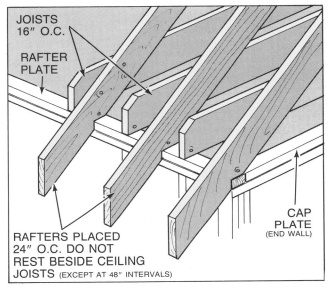

FIGURE C-1-2. Rafters spaced 24″ O.C. cannot be nailed to the side of each ceiling joist.

should be planned so that the rafters and joists can be nailed to each other whenever possible.

The most common spacings between rafters are 16″ O.C. and 24″ O.C. If rafters are spaced 16″ O.C., they will rest beside the ceiling joists, which are normally also placed 16″ O.C. (Figure C-1-1). If 24″ O.C. spacing is used for rafters, a tie-in with ceiling joists will not occur as frequently (Figure C-1-2).

To mark rafter locations when 16″ O.C. spacing is used, proceed as follows:

1. *Mark an X on the outside edge of the end wall, flush with the outside edge.*

   The first rafter pair will be placed atop the double plate, flush with the outside edge of the end wall.

2. *Mark an X on the right-hand side of each ceiling joist.*

   This assumes that the joists have been laid out and installed using the procedures outlined and illustrated in Section C of *Ceiling Framing* (AAVIM, 1990).

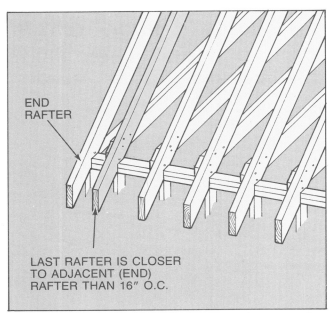

FIGURE C-1-3. The last two rafters may be closer together than other rafters since standard spacing may not be possible.

3. *Place an X at the outside top edge of the cap plate at the other end of the wall frame.*

   The position of the last rafter (the one before the end rafter) may be closer to the adjacent (end) rafter than 16″ since it is at the end of the wall and the standard spacing interval may not be possible (Figure C-1-3).

4. *Repeat steps 1–3 on the other side of the structure, beginning from the same end.*

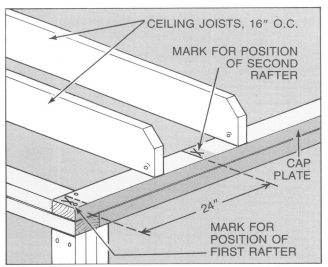

FIGURE C-1-4. If 24″ O.C. spacing is used, mark the position of the second rafter 24″ from the outside edge of the first rafter.

If 24″ O.C. spacing between rafters is planned, proceed as follows:

1. *Mark the position of the first rafter with an X on the end wall, flush with the outside edge.*

2. *Measure 24″ from the outside edge of the first rafter's marked position.*

3. *Make a line across the top plate at the marked point, and mark an X in front of the line (Figure C-1-4).*

   The X indicates the position of the second rafter.

4. *Continue to measure and mark the position of the remaining rafters, 24″ apart.*

   The position of the last rafter may be closer than 24″ from the adjacent (end) rafter since it is located at the end of the wall and standard spacing may not be possible.

5. *Repeat steps 1–4 on the other side of the structure, beginning from the same end.*

2. LAYING OUT AND CUTTING A COMMON RAFTER

All factors involved in determining the length of a common rafter (Section B-3) must be taken into account when you lay out the rafters for a house under construction. Lumber long enough to meet the needs of the situation, yet minimize waste, should be ordered.

For purposes of illustration, the rafters described in Section B-3 will be used as the basis for discussion of layout and cutting. Checking back over Section B-3, you will find that the determined length of the rafters was 15′8″, with another 12″ added as an overhang. A decision was made at that time to purchase 18′ long lumber for these rafters.

Since all common rafters for this roof should be identical in size and length, one pattern rafter can be laid out and cut. Use the pattern to cut your first rafter pair. After these two rafters are cut, test where they sit on the plate and against the ridgeboard (discussed in Section C-3). If a satisfactory fit is achieved, the pattern rafter can act as a template for marking and cutting the remaining rafters.

NOTE: Use the original pattern rafter to mark all other rafters to ensure size consistency. Do not use a piece cut from the pattern. To ensure that the original piece is continually used, mark it on both sides with the word *PATTERN*.

To mark and cut the first pair of rafters, proceed as follows:

1. *Select a piece of rafter lumber from the stock you have ordered, and find the crown edge.*

   All lumber will have a crown or bow along the edge. Rafters should always be installed *crown side up.*

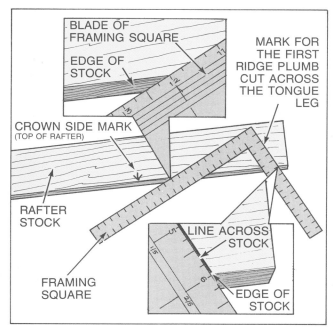

FIGURE C-2-1. Mark the first ridge plumb cut line along the tongue leg of the framing square.

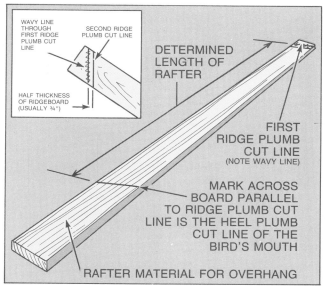

FIGURE C-2-2. The rafter is shortened from the theoretical length (determined body length) to the actual length by drawing a second ridge plumb cut line that allows for half the thickness of the ridgeboard.

2. *Position the lumber across sawhorses with the crown side towards you. Mark the crown side with an arrow (Figure C-2-1).*

3. *Lay a framing square across the right end of the stock, with the tongue leg of the square positioned so that the number corresponding to the stated unit rise (6″ in our example) lies along the crown edge (Figure C-2-1).*

4. *Pivot the blade leg of the framing square so that the 12″ mark is flush with the crown edge (Figure C-2-1).*

   The 12″ mark is used because we are discussing and measuring rise per foot (12″) of run.

5. *Draw a line along the tongue leg edge (Figure C-2-1).*

   This line marks the first **ridge plumb cut**.

6. *Measure and mark a second ridge plumb cut line at a distance from the first line of one half the ridgeboard thickness (¾″ if you are using 1½″-thick ridgeboard).*

   A wavy line should be drawn through the first ridge plumb cut line to avoid confusion when cutting takes place (Figure C-2-2 inset).

   Cutting will be done along the second, straight ridge plumb cut line, which represents **actual rafter length**.

7. *Measure the determined body length of the rafter from the first ridge plumb cut line, and mark this point on the rafter (Figure C-2-2).*

   Determined body length represents **theoretical rafter length**, which was calculated from the center of the ridgeboard. It doesn't include ridgeboard width. Half the ridgeboard width must therefore be subtracted from the determined body length of the rafters on each side of the ridgeboard. This is the purpose of the second ridge plumb cut line in step 6.

8. *Draw a line through the mark, parallel to the ridge plumb cut line (Figure C-2-2).*

   This line marks the **heel plumb cut** for the bird's mouth. The **bird's mouth** is a notch cut into the bottom edge of a rafter in order to provide a flat surface to rest on the top side of the wall's cap plate (Figure C-2-3).

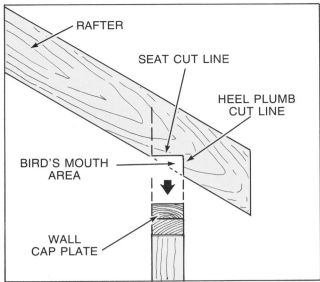

FIGURE C-2-3. The bird's mouth is cut from the bottom of the rafter so the rafters will have a flat seat to rest on top of the wall plate.

9. *Measure a distance equal to the width of the double plate from the heel plumb cut line (3½" in our example), and draw a second line along the right edge of the framing square (Figure C-2-4).*

10. *From the point where the second line meets the bottom edge of the rafter, draw a line at right angles between the parallel lines (Figure C-2-5).*

This line marks the **rafter seat cut** of the bird's mouth (Figure C-2-5).

NOTE: To be sure the strength of the rafter is not affected, at least half the wood of the rafter must be left above the seat cut line. The steeper the

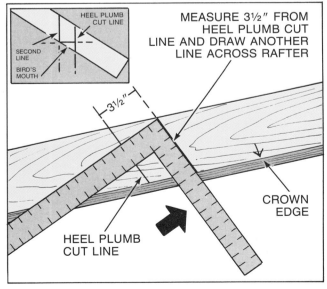

FIGURE C-2-4. The bird's mouth is measured from the heel plumb cut line and is as wide as the double plate (3½" in this example).

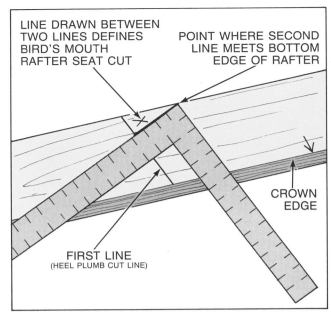

FIGURE C-2-5. After the width has been measured, the rafter seat cut line is marked along the edge of the framing square.

angle of the roof frame, the deeper this cut will be.

11. *Draw an X in the area to be cut out for the bird's mouth (Figure C-2-5).*

12. *Measure down from the heel plumb cut line the distance for the 12" overhang (in this case 13½"), and draw a line across the rafter parallel to the heel plumb cut line (Figure C-2-6).*

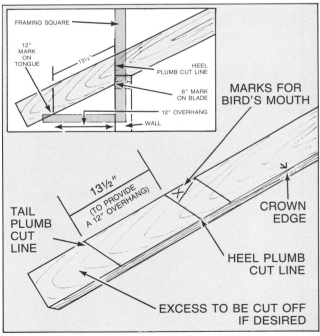

FIGURE C-2-6. The overhang must be measured down the rafter from the heel plumb cut line. Since the rafter runs at an angle, its length is longer than the horizontal width of the overhang. In this example, the rafter length must measure 13½" for a 12" overhang (inset).

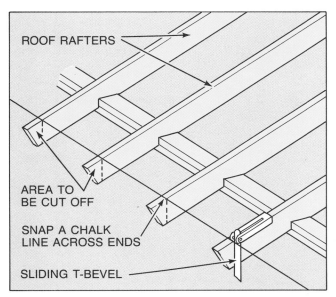

FIGURE C-2-7. A sliding T-bevel can be used to mark the tail plumb cut line on rafters after a chalk line has been snapped across all rafters on one side of the house so all the ends will be even.

This line marks the **tail plumb cut**. Many carpenters choose to measure, mark, and cut off the tail ends from the rafters *after* they are all installed to make alignment of the trimmed edges easier. This is done by snapping a chalk line across the ends of the rafters from one end of the structure to the other. A **sliding T-bevel**—a tool with an adjustable blade that can be locked in any desired position—can be used to mark the tail plumb cut line on each rafter (Figure C-2-7).

You may also make an on-site device called a **poor man's T-bevel** from two pieces of wood and use it to mark the tail plumb cut line (Figure C-2-8).

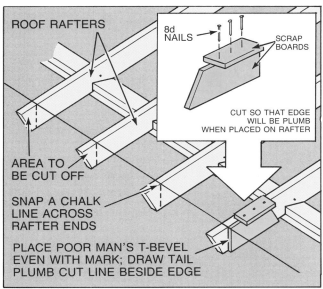

FIGURE C-2-8. A so-called poor man's T-bevel made from two pieces of wood can be helpful in marking the excess on the ends of the rafters.

13. *Cut out your pattern rafter along the marks made on the lumber.*

14. *Use the pattern rafter you created in steps 1–13 to cut out your first rafter pair.*

3. TESTING RAFTERS FOR FIT

Before you cut the total number of rafters needed for the entire roof frame, the first pair of rafters should be checked for fit and accuracy. The subfloor can be used to test the rafters for accuracy and fit if the wall and ceiling framing are not yet in place.

If, however, the step-by-step procedures outlined in the other AAVIM publications in this series (*Floor Framing, Wall Framing,* and *Ceiling Framing*) have been followed, the house now has the floor, wall, and ceiling framing completed. Thus, the testing of the pattern rafters must be made in position on top of the wall framing.

NOTE: All framing procedures should be made with safety as a primary concern. Safety is a particularly important consideration in framing the roof since you will be working in elevated surroundings with lumber and other materials that may be heavy and difficult to handle. Erection of the first pair of rafters—the test rafters or common rafters—should not be attempted with fewer than two persons.

To test rafters for fit, proceed as follows:

1. *Find the center of the end of the house by measuring the width and dividing by 2.*

    The width of the house used as an example throughout this series of publications is 28′. Thus:

    $$\frac{28'}{2} = 14' \text{ center of end of house}$$

2. *Use a chalk line to mark this center position on top of the cap plate at each end of the house and on the ceiling joists.*

3. *Center the end of a 2″ × 4″ temporary prop/spacer over the center mark at one end of the house (Figure C-3-1).*

    The total rise of the roof in our example is 7′. Therefore, a 2″ × 4″ longer than 7′ must be selected to use as a temporary prop and spacer. The actual thickness of a 2″ × 4″ is the same as the thickness of the ridgeboard: 1½″.

4. *Toenail the bottom of the prop to the cap plate (Figure C-3-1).*

5. *Nail a diagonal brace to the side of the prop and to a 2″ × 4″ nailed across two convenient ceiling joists (Figure C-3-1).*

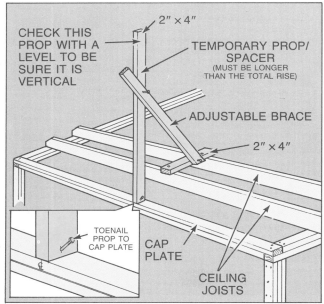

FIGURE C-3-1. A temporary prop/spacer may be installed to test the fit of the first pair of rafters.

6. *Adjust the prop and braces so that the prop is true vertically* (Figure C-3-1).

   Use a plumb bob or 48" spirit level to establish true vertical.

7. *Lift both test rafters into position, and tack or temporarily nail them in place* (Figure C-3-2).

8. *Check each rafter to determine whether the bird's mouth fits properly over the cap plate* (Figure C-3-3a).

   If the fit of the bird's mouth is not satisfactory, make adjustments by remarking and cutting where necessary.

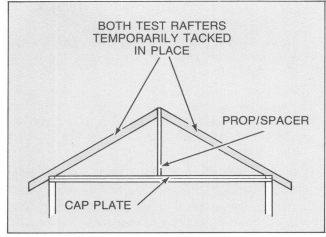

FIGURE C-3-2. The two test rafters (one on each side) should be tacked in position to test (1) the fit of the bird's mouth over the cap plate and (2) the fit of the ridge plumb cut against the prop/spacer.

9. *Check the top end of each rafter to determine whether the ridge plumb cut line is parallel to the prop/spacer and whether the tops of both rafters meet at the same height on the edge of the prop* (Figure C-3-3b).

   If the fit of the ridge plumb cut line is not satisfactory, make adjustments by remarking and cutting where necessary.

10. *Retest the fit.*

    When you are satisfied with the fit, the test rafters can be taken down, the pattern rafter can be adjusted as necessary, and all remaining rafters can be marked and cut.

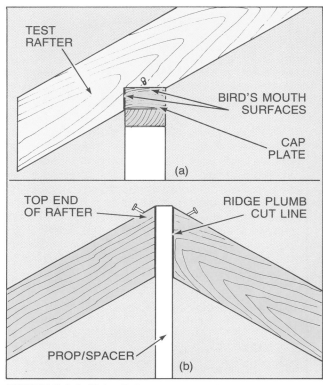

FIGURE C-3-3. If the fit is proper, (a) all bird's mouth surfaces should make good contact with the cap plate; (b) the ridge plumb cut line should be parallel to the prop/spacer.

30

4. SPLICING AND MARKING A RIDGEBOARD

After the rafters have been marked and cut using the pattern rafter, you are ready to assemble the ridgeboard—the horizontal member at the top of the gable roof frame. In Section B-4, materials were figured for its construction for the sample house plan used in this publication.

Remember that the function of the ridgeboard is to provide a way to attach and align the rafters. Therefore, it is important that the ridgeboard be straight.

The ridgeboard of most structures is longer than any one piece of lumber. For instance, the house plan we are using as an example has a roof over 60' long. Therefore, the ridgeboard will have to be made of two or more pieces joined end to end.

Furthermore, it is impractical to make up one continuous ridgeboard and then to lift it into position. Therefore, the ridgeboard should be made in several sections. Unless a heavy beam is being used, the splicing together of at least two pieces of lumber should be accomplished *before* the ridgeboard is put in place.

To splice, raise, and mark a ridgeboard, proceed as follows:

1. *Select two pieces of lumber set aside for the ridgeboard, and square one end of each board.*

2. *Using a level surface as a workplace, butt the squared ends together.*

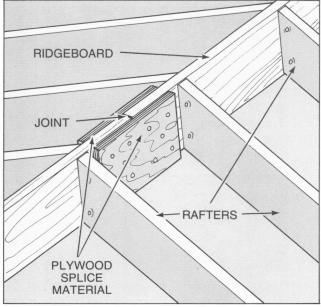

FIGURE C-4-1. Splice boards must be at least 1″ shorter than the planned spacing between rafters so they will not interfere with rafter installation.

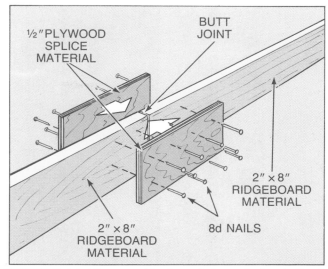

FIGURE C-4-2. The two ridgeboard pieces being spliced must be butted together at the ends, and the splice material (plywood or boards) should be attached to both sides with 8d nails.

3. *Using ½″ plywood or a board the same width as the ridgeboard, cut two splice boards at least 1″ shorter than the planned spacing between rafters.*

   The splice boards should be shorter than the distance between rafters so that they will not interfere with the installation of the rafters (Figure C-4-1).

   NOTE: Metal splice plates can also be used for this purpose.

4. *Place the splice material across the butted joint, and nail to both sides of the boards using ten to twelve 8d nails* (Figure C-4-2).

   Before nailing, make sure that the joint between the ridgeboard material is tight and that the top edge is aligned.

   NOTE: If the splice material is thicker than ½″ plywood, use 16d nails.

5. *Turn the ridgeboard over and repeat the process.*

6. *Lay the ridgeboard across the ceiling joists.*

   Be sure the spliced joint falls between two ceiling joists.

7. *Mark the spacing of the location of rafters on the ridgeboard, as dictated by the location of the installed ceiling joists* (Figure C-4-3).

   This assumes that 16″ O.C. spacing is being used.

This spliced and marked section will be raised into position later, when you are ready to erect the roof frame; and rafters will be nailed to it. Any additional sections of ridgeboard needed will have to be butted, spliced, and marked (steps 1–7) at that time. Note that when the spliced and marked second section is raised into

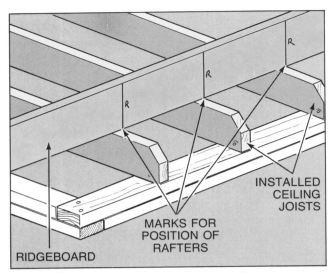

FIGURE C-4-3. The position for the top ends of the rafters (16" O.C.) should be marked on the ridgeboard, using the installed ceiling joists (16" O.C.) as a guide. Use the portion of the joists near the outside wall for greater accuracy.

position, it will have to be spliced to the first section as well.

Remember to leave enough ridgeboard overhanging the end of the house to provide for the framing of the gable overhang. Before installing the first and last sections of ridgeboard, you will need to notch the overhanging portion to match the size of the fascia rafter (Figure C-4-4). The **fascia rafter**—also called a fly rafter, barge rafter, or gable overhang rafter—provides a frame for the overhang of the roof at the end of a gable (Figure A-1-1).

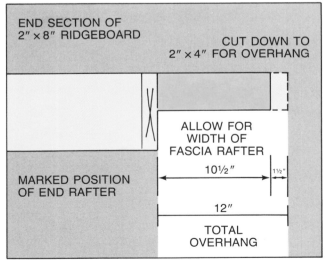

FIGURE C-4-4. The overhanging portion of the ridgeboard at each end of the roof assembly must be cut down to match the size of the fascia rafter. Shown are the measurements used when planning for a 12" overhang.

5. ERECTING A GABLE ROOF FRAME

Once the needed number of rafters have been cut and the ridgeboard spliced and marked, the job of erecting the roof frame may begin.

Remember that safety is very important, and precautions should be taken to prevent accidents. Roof framing is very unstable when it is being erected, and it should not be leaned against or climbed upon until it has been stabilized.

A temporary platform of boards, scaffolding, or sheathing should be provided across the ceiling joists for workers to stand upon during the erection process. Proper, safe scaffolding will save a great deal of time.

Installation procedures differ according to the number of people working on a crew. For purposes of our discussion, the procedures outlined will assume that you are part of a rather small crew of four or fewer persons.

To erect a gable roof frame, proceed as follows:

1. *Position all cut rafters along the rafter plate (at the points marked for their installation) with their tails down on the ground and the ridge plumb cuts up.*

    The rafter plate is the top of the wall's double plate.

2. *Determine the total rise of the roof.*

    From previous discussion, you will recall the total rise for the sample house is 7' (see Section A-2).

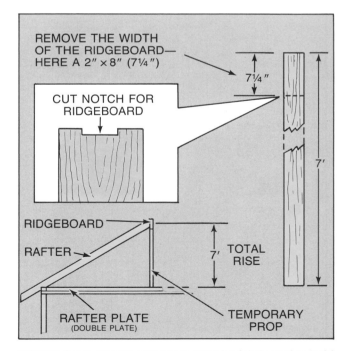

FIGURE C-5-1. Temporary props may be fabricated to hold the ridgeboard in its proper position until it can be secured by the installation of the rafters.

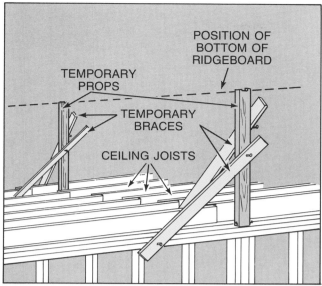

FIGURE C-5-2. Props should be positioned along the path of the ridgeboard at 8' to 10' intervals. They should be checked for correct vertical position and should be properly braced.

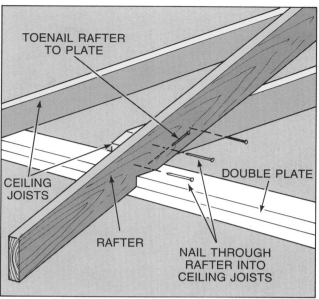

FIGURE C-5-3. Each rafter should be nailed to the double plate and toenailed to the side of a ceiling joist where possible.

3. *Cut enough temporary props so that one can be positioned every 8' to 10' along the bottom of the ridgeboard.*

   Since these temporary props are designed to hold the ridgeboard in place, they will need to be a different length than the one used to test common rafters (see Section C-3).

   In order to cut props of the proper length, deduct the width of the ridgeboard from the 7' total rise height. You may also wish to make a shallow notch in the top of the prop for the ridgeboard to rest on (Figure C-5-1).

4. *Install the vertical props every 8' to 10' along the area where the ridgeboard will be raised, brace each one with two temporary braces, and adjust the braces until each prop is plumb (Figure C-5-2).*

   Braces can be attached to the ceiling joists or to the rafter plates (double plates) on the partition walls, using 10d–16d nails.

5. *Set the ridgeboard on top of the temporary props.*

   Again, safety is a primary concern, so as the ridgeboard is raised by one group of carpenters/students, it should be steadied by another group of carpenters/students working at the top end of the rafter-nailing position (ridgeboard).

6. *Line up the ridge plumb cut of the first rafter with the mark drawn on the ridgeboard at the end wall. Set the seat cut of the rafter on the rafter plate (double plate). Secure both ends in place.*

   First, toenail the bottom end of the rafter to the rafter plate and nail it to the side of a ceiling joist with 16d nails (Figure C-5-3). Next, tacknail the top end of the rafter to the ridgeboard. Tacknailing will allow you to shift the position of the rafter slightly if needed.

   If the spacing between rafters is 24" O.C., most rafters will not be positioned where they can be nailed to the sides of ceiling joists. Therefore, you will need to use metal rafter brackets to secure the lower end of each rafter.

7. *Lift into position the rafter on the opposite side of the ridgeboard, and secure it to the rafter plate and ridgeboard.*

   NOTE: The tops of each pair of rafters on opposite sides of the ridgeboard may fit on opposite sides of the marking made for placement of the ridge plumb cut ends. If, for example, the ceiling joists are laid out so they overlap on the center wall and the rafters are positioned by the sides of the joists, the rafter ends will be offset on the ridgeboard (Figure C-5-4). Because of the offset of the rafters, there will be a problem with the installation of the collar beams (See Section C-6).

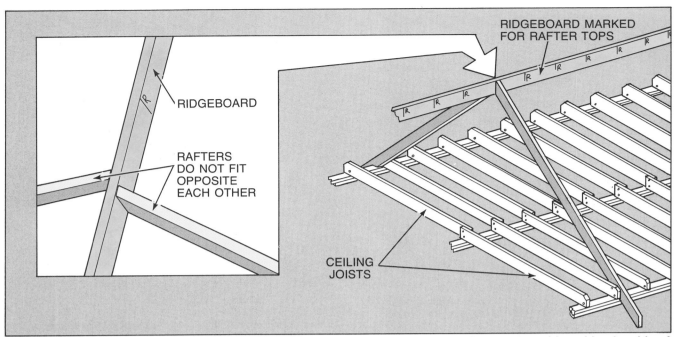

FIGURE C-5-4. Rafter tops will not meet opposite each other on the ridgeboard if they are positioned by the side of ceiling joists that have been lapped over a central support wall without any spacer provision.

8. *Add temporary braces as needed to steady and straighten the roof assembly.*

   These braces, generally made of 1″ × 4″ or 2″ × 4″ pieces, may be nailed across the bottoms of the rafters diagonally, usually at mid-span. Braces may also be installed between the ceiling joists and ridgeboard to ensure correct position of the components. Rafters may need to be further straightened when the decking (sheathing) is attached.

9. *Repeat steps 6 to 8 at the other end of the propped-up section of ridgeboard with another set of rafters.*

10. *Add sets of rafters on either side of any splices and as additional sections of the ridgeboard are installed.*

    NOTE: As rafters are added, the ridgeboard should be checked with a level, and any necessary adjustments should be made. Adjustments may require movement of temporary braces already in place or the use of additional braces.

    There is another method used by some carpenters to check the level and straightness of the ridgeboard as it and the roof assembly are being constructed. The props at either end of the roof assembly are modified so that one side of each prop is as high as the total rise of the roof. These props are checked for accuracy of position and secured with temporary braces

Masonry twine or nylon string is then fastened between the end props, pulled out, and checked for levelness with a line level. As the rafters and ridgeboard are installed, the taut line serves as a guide for determining the straightness of the ridgeboard (Figure C-5-5).

11. *Install all other common rafters in pairs along the ridgeboard as outlined in steps 6 and 7, continually checking the level and straightness of the roof frame assembly as you install each set of rafters.*

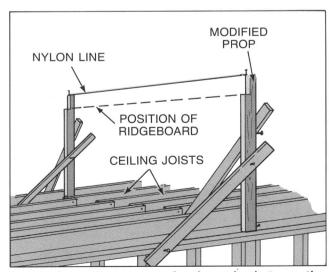

FIGURE C-5-5. You can stretch nylon string between the end props, pull it taut, check it for levelness, and use it as a guide for checking the straightness of the ridgeboard.

34

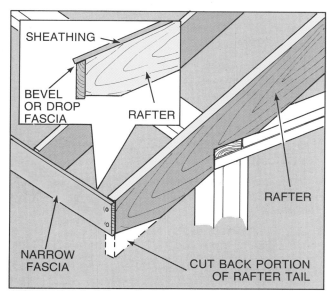

FIGURE C-5-6. If the tail of the rafter is cut back, narrower finished fascia board can be used. The fascia should be beveled on the top or dropped down so it will not interfere with the fit of the sheathing when it is installed atop the rafters (inset).

12. *Nail the finished fascia board to the tail end of the installed rafters.*

A **finished fascia board** is a finished piece of lumber that is nailed to the tail ends of the rafters or to a rough fascia (see NOTE below). Lumber that is 1″ thick (nominal) and at least one size wider than the rafter material should be used.

Wider lumber is generally required because the angular tail cut of the rafter is longer than the width of the rafter. Narrower fascia board can be used, however, if the tail end of the rafter is cut back (Figure C-5-6).

Whether narrow or wide fascia is installed, you must be sure to position the top of the material so that it will not interfere with the sheathing when it is installed (Figure C-5-6). Remember to leave enough lumber extending beyond the end rafter to allow for the gable overhang framing (discussed in Section D).

NOTE: Some carpenters attach a **rough fascia board** to the ends of the rafter before attaching the finished fascia. The rough fascia is generally the same thickness as the rafters. The finished fascia is then generally installed along the overhang during the finish and trim phase of construction, which comes later.

6. INSTALLING COLLAR BEAMS (OR TIES)

In many areas, local codes require an additional support or brace in the roof framing. This member, installed on either every second or third set of rafters, is called a **collar beam** or **collar tie**. Constructed of a 1″ × 6″, 2″ × 4″, or 2″ × 6″ piece of lumber, it connects two opposite rafters.

Collar beams are installed to strengthen the roof frame. They act as tension members to keep the rafters from spreading apart. They are especially important in the roof framing of houses with low pitch. The lower the angle, the greater the force to push the rafters outward.

To install collar beams, proceed as follows:

1. *Count the number of rafter sets and divide by two or three depending upon the spacing you decide upon.*

   For purposes of illustration, assume there are 45 sets of rafters and that a collar beam will be installed on every third set of rafters:

   $$\frac{45}{3} = 15 \text{ collar beams needed}$$

2. *Mark a pair of rafters so that the distance from the bottom of the ridgeboard to the top of the collar beam position will be 18″ to 24″ (Figure C-6-1).*

   Collar beams should be installed in the upper third of the roof framing. If there are no specific directions on your plans, position them as described above.

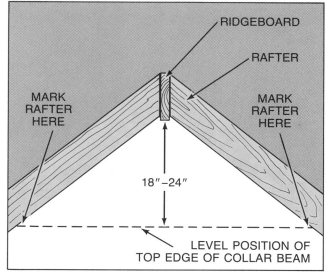

FIGURE C-6-1. Collar beams should be installed in the top third of the roof framing, generally 18″ to 24″ from the bottom of the ridgeboard.

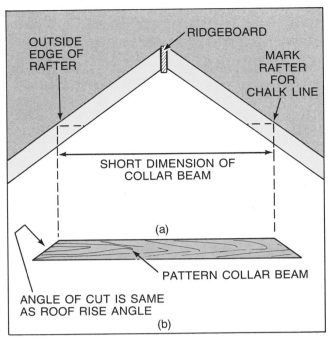

FIGURE C-6-2. (a) Measure the distance between the outside edges of the rafter at the point where the rafters are marked to determine the short dimension of the collar beam. (b) Mark a board with the short measurement and draw a line at the same angle as the roof rise to the outside of each mark.

3. *From the marks on the rafters, measure the distance between the outside edges of the rafters (Figure C-6-2a).*

This measurement will be the *short* dimension of the beam.

4. *Mark a board with this measurement, and draw a line at the angle of the roof rise to the outside of both marks (Figure C-6-2b).*

You should know the angle of roof rise from information obtained when marking, cutting, and installing the rafters.

NOTE: Although this cut does not have to be exact, the ends should be trimmed at the roof angle to provide maximum surface for nailing the beam to the rafters.

5. *When these marks are completed, cut the board and test the pattern collar beam for fit. Make adjustments as needed.*

6. *Using the pattern beam, cut the required number of collar beams from 1″ x 6″, 2″ x 4″, or 2″ x 6″ stock.*

7. *Nail a collar beam in place at either end of the roof frame using 10d or 16d nails. Position each beam so that the tops of its cut edges are at or near the top edges of the rafters.*

8. *Chalk a line across the tops of the rafters on each side of the ridgeboard to indicate the placement of the remaining collar beams.*

Start the chalk line at the point where the collar beam at one end of the roof assembly intersects the rafter on one side of the ridgeboard. Stretch the chalk line to the same point on the collar beam at the other end of the house. Then snap the line. Repeat for the rafters on the other side of the ridgeboard.

9. *Using the chalked lines as a guide, nail the remaining collar beams in place with 10d or 16d nails.*

7. INSTALLING BRACES TO HELP SUPPORT RAFTERS

Rafters should also be supported from beneath with braces. The flatter the pitch, the greater the need for additional support. Flatter roofs have a greater tendency to spread apart than do steeper pitched roofs.

The needed support can be provided by a series of 2″ × 4″ **knee braces**, which extend from a load-bearing wall or plate across the ceiling joists to the bottoms or sides of the rafters (Figure C-7-1). The support will be greatest if the braces are located near mid-span. This will help prevent the sagging of long rafters.

To install braces from a load-bearing wall or plate, proceed as follows:

1. *Starting on one side of the house, chalk a line across the bottom of the rafters at mid-span, and use 16d nails to nail a 2″ × 4″ purlin to the bottom side of the rafters along the line. Repeat on the other side of the house.*

2. *Starting on one side of the house, chalk a line across the ceiling joists near mid-span, and use 16d nails to nail a 2″ × 4″ plate across the line. Repeat on the other side of the house.*

3. *Make a pattern knee brace by placing a 2″ × 4″ between the plate and the purlin across the bottom of the rafters and marking the angle cut, top and bottom.*

4. *Use the pattern brace to cut enough knee braces for the roof assembly.*

   If the rafters are placed 16″ O.C., you will need one brace for every third rafter (on each side). Rafters spaced 24″ O.C. will require one brace for every other rafter (on each side).

5. *Toenail the braces to the purlins (at the top) and to the plate (at the bottom) with 16d nails.*

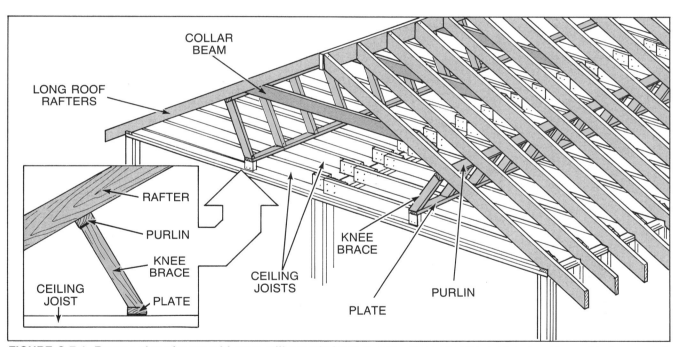

FIGURE C-7-1. Braces placed near mid-span will greatly increase the strength of a roof assembly and help prevent sagging of the rafters.

STUDY QUESTIONS

Part I: Labeling

The lumber below has been marked as a pattern rafter. Identify each of the ten numbered parts, and write each response in the corresponding space provided below.

1. _____

2. _____

3. _____

4. _____

5. _____

6. _____

7. _____

8. _____

9. _____

10. _____

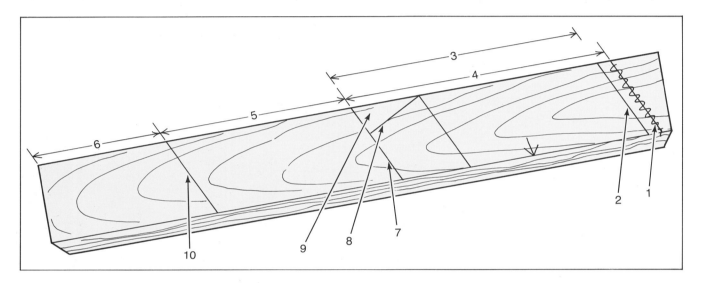

Part II: Short Answer

1. Rafters are nailed at the bottom end to the rafter plate (wall plate, double plate). To what other framing component should rafter bottoms be nailed whenever possible?

2. Standard spacing (e.g., 16″, 24″) might not be possible between which **two** rafters?

3. Should rafters be installed with the crown side up or down?

4. What type of tool should be used to mark the tail plumb cut line on each rafter once installed?

5. In testing rafters for fit, what device serves as a "ridgeboard"?

6. What is the minimum number of people who should be involved in erecting rafters?

7. What part of each test rafter should fit properly against (make good contact with) the cap plate?

8. What part of each test rafter should fit properly against (be parallel to) the prop/spacer?

9. The length of the splice boards used to join ridgeboard sections should be 1″ shorter than what?

10. Vertical props are used to hold the ridgeboard temporarily in place. How many feet should there be between these props? (Give a range.)

11. On what should workers stand in order to be safe when they are erecting a gable roof frame?

12. As rafters are erected and secured, why must the ridgeboard be continually checked?

13. Which has a greater need for additional support: a flatter roof or a steeper roof?

14. Collar beams and knee braces keep the rafters from doing what?

15. In what section of the roof framing should collar beams be installed?

16. Knee braces are nailed at one end to a 2″ × 4″ secured to the bottom side of the rafters. What is that 2″ × 4″ called?

Most houses with gable roofs are designed so that the roof extends beyond the end wall. This extension is known as a **gable end overhang** (or **rake**). The framing for this addition is done after the common rafters are in place and have been checked for straightness.

The framing in this area involves framing the triangular area between the double plate and the rafters known as the **gable end**.

Framing a gable end overhang and gable end is discussed under the following headings:

1. Framing a Gable End Overhang
2. Framing a Gable End

1. FRAMING A GABLE END OVERHANG

The extension framing for a gable end overhang resembles a ladder that has been laid beside the rafters overhanging the wall. The pieces making up this framing are known by special names and will be explained or defined as the discussion progresses.

To frame a gable end overhang, proceed as follows:

1. *Determine the width of the overhang.*

    Your house plans should give you this information.

2. *Using rafter stock, cut two rafters just like the common rafters for the roof except for the bird's mouth. No bird's mouth should be cut out of either rafter.*

    These rafters, located at the outside edge of the overhang framing, are called **fascia rafters**, **fly rafters**, **bargeboards**, **barge rafters**, or **gable overhang rafters** (Figure D-1-1).

3. *On the end rafters, measure off spacing for the position of the lookouts and stiffeners at either 16" or 24" intervals, and mark the locations.*

    The **lookouts**, also called **outriggers**, **ladder steps**, or **lookout braces**, are the horizontal pieces that project beyond the exterior wall of the structure. The **stiffeners** are the longer lookouts that extend from the second common rafter, over

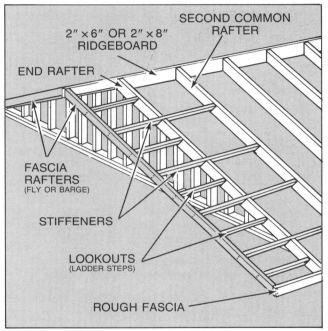

FIGURE D-1-1. The rafters at the outside edge of the overhang at the end of the roof have no bird's mouth and are called fascia rafters, fly rafters, bargeboards, barge rafters, or gable overhang rafters.

the notched end rafter, and out to the side of the fascia rafter. The purpose of lookouts and stiffeners is to provide a support for the fascia rafter as well as a nailing surface for the soffit finish material.

4. *Determine the length of the lookouts and stiffeners.*

    Before you can begin to figure and mark lumber, you will need to know how many stiffeners and how many lookouts will be needed. Every other lookout should be a stiffener if your spacing between lookouts is 24" O.C. Every third lookout should be a stiffener for 16" O.C. spacing.

    In order to correctly figure the length of the stiffeners, you must add (a) the length of the overhang, (b) the distance to the second common

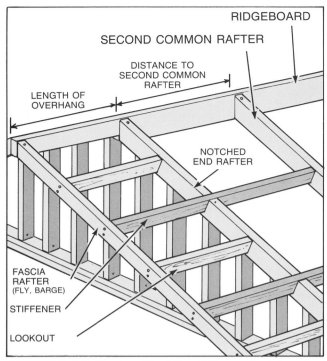

FIGURE D-1-2. The length of the stiffeners is determined by figuring the distance between the inside of the fascia rafter and the outside edge of the second common rafter.

rafter, and (c) the width of the fascia rafter. The length of the short lookouts is the same as the length of the overhang (Figure D-1-2).

5. *From 2" × 4" material, cut the number and length of lookouts and stiffeners needed.*

6. *Notch the end rafters (first common rafters) at the marked locations for the stiffeners.*

   Notches should be 3½" deep and 1½" wide to accommodate a 2" × 4" (nominal) stiffener turned on edge.

7. *Nail the stiffeners to the side of the second rafter and to the notched end rafter with three 16d nails (Figure D-1-3).*

8. *Lift each fascia rafter into position, and nail it to the ridgeboard at the top and to the fascia board at the bottom with 10d nails.*

   When several carpenters are working together, some supervisors prefer to construct the overhang assembly on the ground. All lookouts and a few of the stiffeners are nailed to the fascia rafter, and then the entire assembly is raised and nailed in place.

9. *Nail through the side of the fascia rafters into the ends of the lookouts and stiffeners with 16d nails.*

   As you nail, be sure that the top edges of the fascia rafters and the lookouts and stiffeners are even.

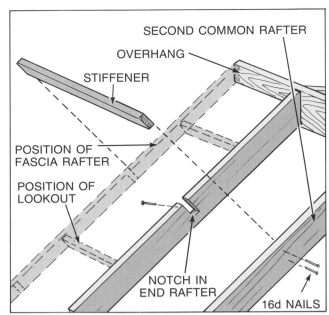

FIGURE D-1-3. The stiffeners are nailed to the side of the second rafter and are nailed into the notch on top of the end rafter.

10. *Install the lookouts between the fascia rafters and the end rafters, and nail through the side of the rafters into the ends of the lookouts.*

11. *After all the pieces are nailed in place, trim any excess ridgeboard and fascia length beyond the fascia rafter.*

   You may recall that the width of the ridgeboard was cut down earlier to match the width of the fascia rafter (Figure C-4-4). These pieces can also be measured and cut to length on the ground before erection of the assembly.

2. FRAMING A GABLE END

The gable end framing is constructed after the rafters have been installed and the roof assembly has been checked for straightness. The gable end assembly can then be built to fit exactly the triangular spaces at the ends of the roof framing.

Although there are several ways to frame a gable end, the method described here assumes that the roof frame has been installed and checked for accuracy, that the roof assembly has an overhang and an end rafter, and that space has been left for a prebuilt louvered gable vent assembly.

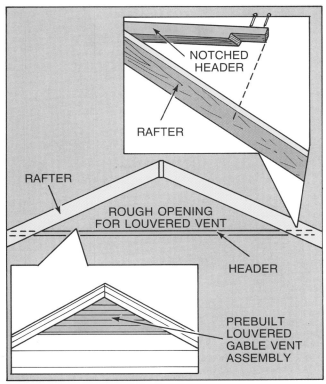

FIGURE D-2-1. A header must be installed between the rafters to accommodate the vent assembly and provide a nailing surface for the tops of gable studs.

To frame a gable end, proceed as follows:

1. *Starting from the bottom of the ridgeboard, measure down the distance required for a rough opening for a prebuilt louvered gable vent assembly.*

   To determine these dimensions, take measurements from the assembly on the job site, and consult a building supply catalog or a representative of the company from which you buy building materials.

2. *Cut a 2" × 4" header long enough to span the area between the rafters on opposite sides.*

   Figure enough length to include the width of the rafters at the point where the header and the rafters will intersect (Figure D-2-1).

   NOTE: The header can be toenailed to the bottom side of the rafters. However, a stronger header can be produced by notching the ends of the header so there will be a greater nailing surface (Figure D-2-1).

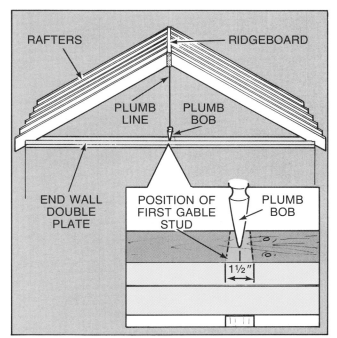

FIGURE D-2-2. A plumb line dropped from the center of the bottom of the ridgeboard will indicate the position of the first gable stud.

3. *Nail the header in place with 16d nails.*

4. *Drop a plumb line from the center of the end of the ridgeboard, and mark the position on the double plate of the end wall (Figure D-2-2).*

   This mark indicates the position of the first **gable stud**.

5. *From the line denoting the position of the first stud, measure outward in both directions at 16" intervals (16" O.C.) for the positions of the remaining studs in the gable (Figure D-2-3).*

6. *Measure the vertical distance between the double plate and the bottom of the header you've installed to find the length of the studs needed in this area of the gable end (Figure D-2-3).*

   After you determine the correct length, cut a sample stud and put it in position to check the fit.

7. *Determine the number of studs needed of this same length, and cut them from 2" × 4" stock.*

8. *Install these common-length studs by toenailing them to the double plate at the bottom and nailing through the header into their top ends.*

   Check the plumb of each stud with a level.

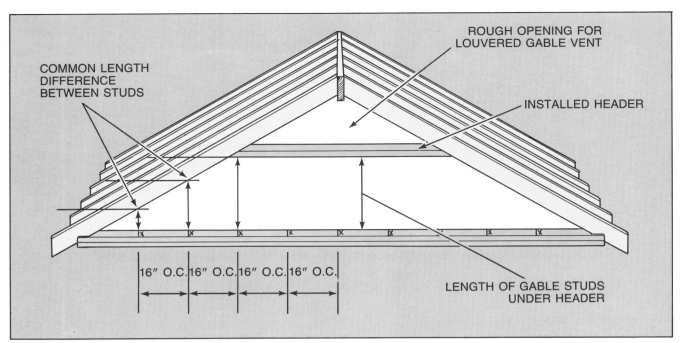

FIGURE D-2-3. The length of studs beneath the header is the distance between the bottom of the header and the double plate. The distance between studs should be marked at 16″ O.C. intervals, beginning at the center stud location.

9. *Calculate the common length difference of the remaining studs.*

The remaining studs in each half of the gable will be of different lengths. In Section B-5, procedures

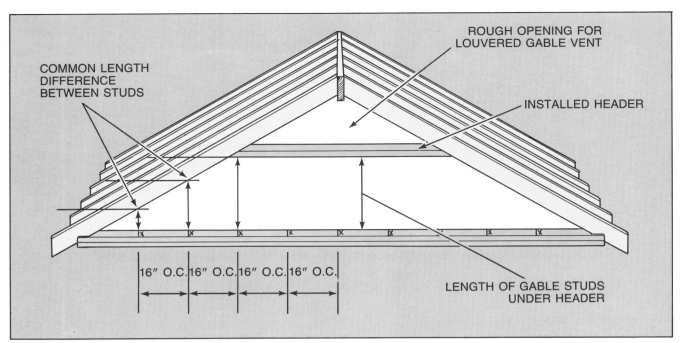

FIGURE D-2-4. Gable studs can be toenailed to the bottom of the rafter (left inset) or notched out and nailed to the sides of the rafter (right inset).

were discussed for finding the *common length difference* of these studs using a framing square.

Another method for finding this difference is to multiply the unit rise of the roof by the spacing of the studs in feet. The model house we've been building has a unit rise of 6″ and the spacing between gable studs is 16″ O.C. (or 1.333′). Thus:

$$\begin{array}{r} 1.333 \\ \times\ 6 \\ \hline 7.998'' \end{array}$$ or 8″ common length difference

This common length difference means that each gable stud will be shorter than the next longest stud by 8″ (Figure D-2-3).

These studs that decrease in length as their position gets closer to the edge of the roof are also called **gable jacks**. In a symmetrical gable, there will always be four jacks or studs of the same length—one on each side at each end—but two with the angled cut reversed. If a carpenter happens to cut the wrong angle, the gable jack or stud can possibly be used on the other side or other end of the roof frame.

10. *Calculate the length of the remaining studs needed.*

When making calculations for the first stud beyond those under any header for vents, it is best to add enough length to allow for notching the stud to fit around the rafter. Although shorter studs can be cut, fitted, and toenailed to the bottom edge of the end rafter, the longer notched stud is stronger and attaches more easily (Figure D-2-4).

To calculate the length of this first notched stud, measure from the top of the cap plate to the *top*

42

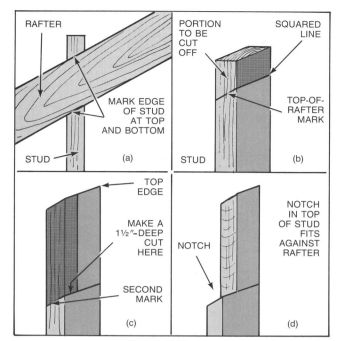

FIGURE D-2-5. Starting with the longest stud, (a) place material on end and mark the position of the top and bottom of the rafter on the edge of stud; (b) draw squared lines across the side of the stud at both marks, and cut off the end of the stud along the top mark; (c) make a 1½"-deep cut at the second mark; and (d) draw a line between the trim edge and the 1½" cut, and cut along that line to complete the notch.

of the end rafter. Start with the longest stud in the gable beyond those under the header and work to the shortest.

11. *Cut the first stud, and set it (on end) on the designated mark on the double plate. Plumb it with a level. Mark the position of the top and bottom of the rafter on the edge of the stud (Figure D-2-5a).*

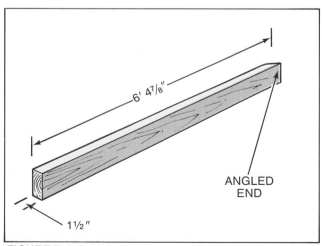

FIGURE D-2-6. Make a pattern gable stud for the first angled end stud at each end of the house.

12. *Square the lines across the face of the stud (Figure D-2-5b).*

13. *Cut off the top of the stud at the same angle as the top mark on the edge of the stud.*

14. *At the second mark (the bottom edge of the rafter) make a cut 1½" deep at the same angle as the mark (Figure D-2-5c).*

    The depth of this cut equals the thickness of the rafter.

15. *Complete the notch by drawing a line from the top edge of the stud down to the 1½" cut just made and cutting along that line (Figure D-2-5d).*

16. *Cut all remaining studs, and install them along the double plate according to the spacing marks already made.*

17. *Repeat the procedure for the gable at the opposite end of the roof.*

There is an alternate method of cutting the gable studs. Proceed as follows:

1. *Make a pattern stud for the first full angled stud (first stud to either side of the center stud).*

   In the sample house, this pattern stud would be 6'4⅞" (Figure D-2-6).

2. *Starting from the bottom end of the pattern stud, make marks at intervals equal to the common length difference between studs—8" in our example (Figure D-2-7).*

   The size of the interval will vary with roof pitch and other factors associated with any particular house.

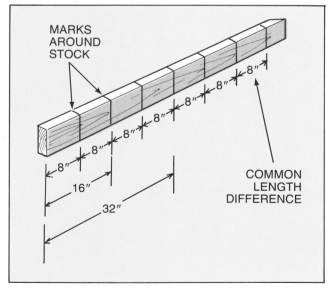

FIGURE D-2-7. Place marks around the stock at intervals equal to the common length difference for the gable you are constructing.

43

3. *Using the pattern stud, measure and mark studs in the number and length needed.*

4. *Cut the studs as you mark them using the pattern stud.*

   Start with the longest studs and work down to the shortest to minimize waste.

STUDY QUESTIONS

---

1. What do fascia rafters, fly rafters, bargeboards, barge rafters, and gable overhang rafters have in common?

2. How are the rafters for the gable end overhang different from the common rafters for the roof?

3. What type of construction equipment does the extension framing for a gable overhang resemble?

4. Shorter lookouts extend from the fascia rafter to what framing component?

5. Stiffeners (longer lookouts) extend from the fascia rafter to what framing component?

6. What is done to the end rafters to accommodate the stiffeners?

7. If your spacing is 16" O.C., how many lookouts should be stiffeners?

8. If your spacing is 24" O.C., how many lookouts should be stiffeners?

9. What prebuilt component goes at the top of gable end triangle?

10. What purpose is served by notching the ends of the header that supports the prebuilt component from below?

11. A plumb line is used to mark the position of the first gable stud on the double plate. From what point is the plumb line dropped?

12. **True or False.** Gable studs under the header are all one common length; gable studs on either side of the header decrease in length by a common length difference as their position gets closer to the edge of the roof.

E.

Laying Out, Cutting & Installing Rafters for a Hip Roof

Earlier sections of this publication have discussed the procedures involved in building a gable roof assembly. Although gable roofs are the most commonly built roofs, hip roofs are also very popular.

A **hip roof** is a roof that slopes downward in four directions from one central ridgeboard (Figure E-1).

Laying out, cutting, and installing rafters for a hip roof is described under the following headings:

1. Parts of a Basic Hip Roof Frame
2. Determining the Length of the Ridgeboard for a Hip Roof
3. Determining the Length of a Hip Rafter
4. Laying Out and Cutting a Hip Rafter
5. Backing or Dropping Hip Rafters
6. Laying Out and Cutting Jack Rafters
7. Erecting a Hip Roof Frame

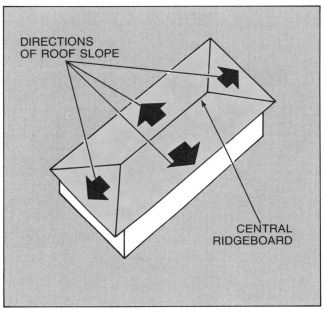

FIGURE E-1. A hip roof slopes downward in four directions from the ridgeboard.

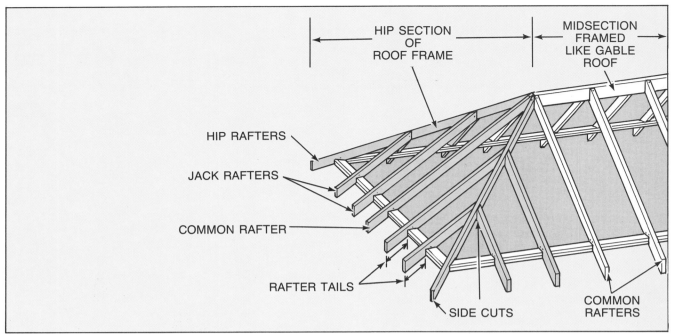

HIP SECTION OF ROOF FRAME

MIDSECTION FRAMED LIKE GABLE ROOF

HIP RAFTERS

JACK RAFTERS

COMMON RAFTER

RAFTER TAILS

SIDE CUTS

COMMON RAFTERS

FIGURE E-1-1. The ends of a hip roof assembly are constructed of unique components that are figured, cut, and installed differently from the central section.

1. PARTS OF A BASIC HIP ROOF FRAME

The central section of a hip roof and a gable roof are framed in the same way and the terms used are the same. The differences between gable and hip roof framing occur in the construction at the ends of the roof frame assembly (Figure E-1-1).

The following terms are unique to hip roof framing:

Hip rafter—rafter that extends diagonally downward from the ridgeboard to the outside corner of an exterior wall (Figure E-1-1).

Jack rafters (also known as **hip jack rafters** or **cripple jack rafters**)—shortened rafters that do not extend the full length from the double plate to the ridgeboard (Figure E-1-1).

Side cut (also called a **cheek cut**)—angular, beveled cut (or cuts) made on the ends of a hip rafter or jack rafter. Angled cuts allow you to join a roof member (e.g., jack rafter) to an angled member (e.g., hip rafter) or to fit a roof member (e.g., hip rafter) into an angled area (Figure E-1-2).

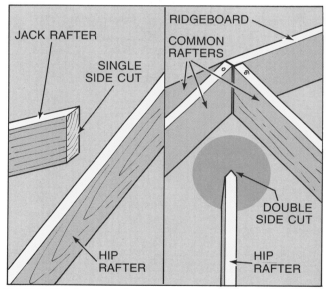

JACK RAFTER

SINGLE SIDE CUT

RIDGEBOARD

COMMON RAFTERS

HIP RAFTER

DOUBLE SIDE CUT

HIP RAFTER

FIGURE E-1-2. Angled cuts must be made at the ends of rafters in a hip roof when joining angled pieces. These cuts are known as side cuts or cheek cuts. They may be (a) single side cuts or (b) double side cuts.

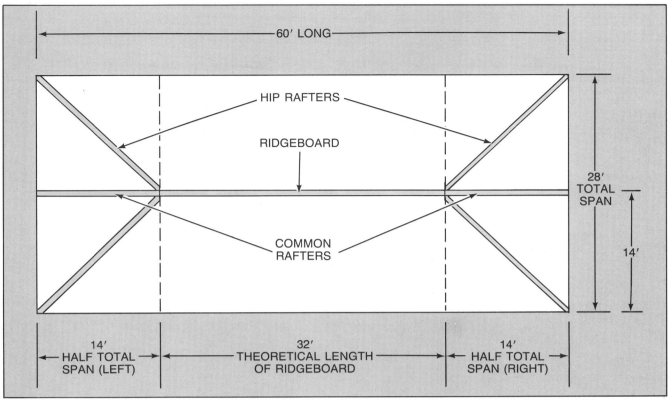

FIGURE E-2-1. The theoretical length of the ridgeboard can be found by subtracting the total span (28') from the total length (60'). One half of the span (14') is deducted from each end of the house.

2. DETERMINING THE LENGTH OF THE RIDGEBOARD FOR A HIP ROOF

You need to know the actual length of the ridgeboard before you can estimate the materials needed. To find the *theoretical* and *actual* length of a ridgeboard, proceed as follows:

1. *Take the length of the house (in feet) and subtract the roof's total span (in feet).*

   The house we will use in our example is 60' long, with a total span of 28'. Thus:

   $$\begin{array}{r} 60' \\ -\ 28' \\ \hline 32' \end{array}$$ theoretical length of ridgeboard

   NOTE: One half the total span of the roof will be divided between the left and right ends of the house (Figure E-2-1).

2. *If a common rafter is to be placed at the center of the hip at each end, increase the theoretical length of the ridgeboard by one half the thickness of each of the two common rafters* (Figure E-2-2).

   The thickness of each common rafter is 1½". Half of that would be ¾". Thus:

   $$\begin{array}{r} 32' \\ +\quad ¾'' \\ +\quad ¾'' \\ \hline 32'1½'' \end{array}$$ actual length of ridgeboard

   NOTE: When this arrangement is used, the common rafter also acts as a brace.

47

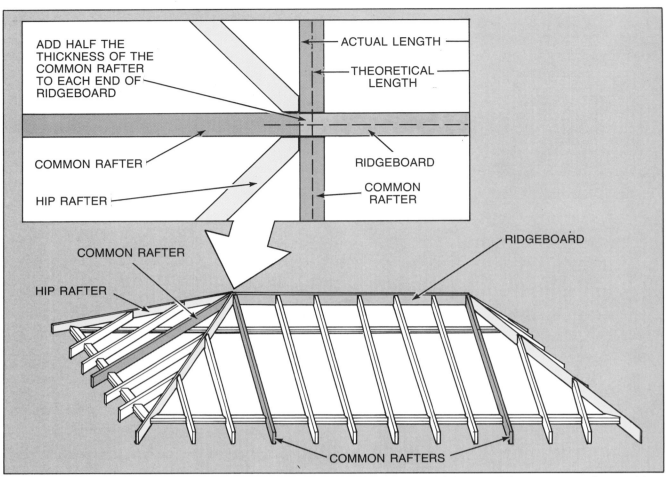

FIGURE E-2-2. To find the actual length of the ridgeboard, add one half the thickness of the common rafter at either end of the roof to the theoretical length.

3. DETERMINING THE LENGTH OF A HIP RAFTER

There are several differences between common rafters and hip rafters. For one thing, hip rafters are longer than common rafters since they reach the ridgeboard by traveling upward at a 45° angle from the corners of the double plate (rafter plate).

Hip rafters also require side cuts (or cheek cuts) at the point where they meet the ridgeboard, as well as at the tail cut end so that the overhang will align with the ends of the common rafters.

In addition, the unit run for a hip rafter is longer (17") than that of a common rafter (12"). Because a hip rafter runs at a 45° angle to the common rafter, the unit run is figured by taking the diagonal measurement of a 12" square (Figure E-3-1).

The diagonal distance is 16.97" or, rounded off, 17". This means that a hip rafter must cover or travel 17" to reach the same height that a common rafter would travel in 12" (Figure E-3-1).

Although there are several methods for determining the length of hip rafters, including the use of a book of printed rafter tables, the method described here assumes the use of a steel framing square with a stamped or etched rafter table.

Use of the first line on this tool to determine the length and marking of common rafters was discussed in Section C-2. The first line shows the length of **common rafters** per foot of run.

The framing square can be used in determining the length of hip rafters by using the second line on the blade, which provides the correct figures for length of **hip rafters** per foot of run.

To find the length of a hip rafter for the house used as an example in this publication, which is 28' wide with a unit rise of 6" per foot, proceed as follows:

1. *Divide the total span of the house (28') by 2 to find the total run.*

$$\frac{28}{2} = 14' \text{ total run}$$

48

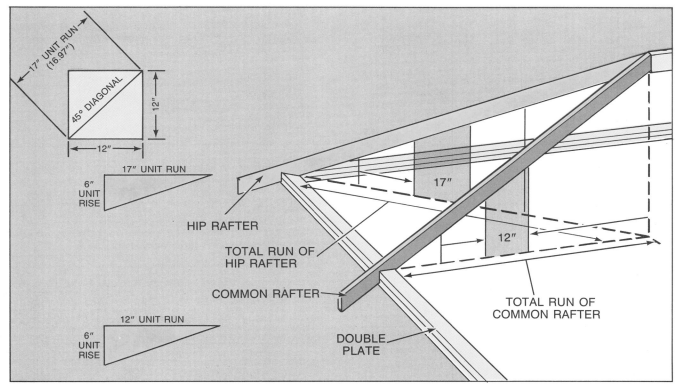

FIGURE E-3-1. Hip rafters are longer than common rafters. Because they travel upward at a 45° angle, they take 17″ to cover the distance that a common rafter would cover in 12″.

2. *Take the framing square, and locate the number corresponding to the stated unit rise (6″) on the blade (the 24″ leg). Find the corresponding number on the second line.*

   The number you will find on the second line below the 6″ mark is 18.00, which is the length (in inches) of the hip rafter per foot of run for a roof with a 6″ unit rise.

3. *Multiply the number of feet in the total run (14) by the length of hip rafter per foot of run (18″).*

$$\begin{array}{r} 18'' \\ \times\,14 \\ \hline 72 \\ 18 \\ \hline 252'' \end{array}$$
   determined length of hip rafters (in inches)

4. *Divide the total (252″) by 12 (the number of inches in a foot) to determine the length of the hip rafter in feet.*

   $$\frac{252''}{12} = 21'$$ determined length of hip rafter (in feet)

5. *To determine the length to be added for the overhang, first multiply the number of inches of overhang of the common rafters by 1.42″—the distance a hip rafter overhang must extend beyond the double plate for every 1″ a common rafter extends.*

Since our sample house has an overhang of 12″, multiply 12″ × 1.42″ to determine the length of overhang of the hip rafter:

$$\begin{array}{r} 1.42'' \\ \times\,12'' \\ \hline 284 \\ 142 \\ \hline 17.04'' \end{array}$$
length of overhang

NOTE: The allowance for overhang (beyond the double plate) must be added to the length of the hip rafter because, unlike the common rafter, it runs at a diagonal.

6. *Add this total (17.04″) to the determined length (in inches) of the hip rafter (252″).*

$$\begin{array}{r} 252.00'' \\ +\,17.04'' \\ \hline 269.04'' \end{array}$$

7. *Divide the total (269.04″) by 12 (the number of inches in a foot).*

   $$\frac{269.04''}{12} = 22.42'$$

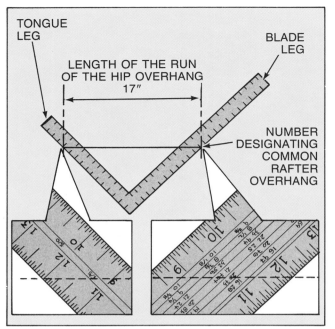

FIGURE E-3-2. The framing square can be used to determine the length of lumber needed so the overhang of the hip rafter will match that of the common rafters.

8. *Convert the total feet into inches by multiplying the decimal fraction (.42) by 12 (the number of inches in a foot) and then rounding to the next highest whole number.*

$$\begin{array}{r} .42 \\ \times 12 \\ \hline 84 \\ 42 \\ \hline 5.04'' \end{array}$$, rounded to 6''

Thus, the hip rafter in our example should have a total length of 22'6".

There is an alternate method for calculating the run of the hip rafter overhang (step 5 above), which involves the use of a steel framing square. Proceed as follows:

1. *Turn the framing square so that the short leg (tongue) is on your left and the long leg (blade) is on your right (Figure E-3-2).*

2. *Identify the number of inches of overhang of the common rafters, and locate that number on the outside of each leg of the framing square.*

   In our sample house, this number would be 12" (Figure E-3-2).

3. *Measure, diagonally, the distance from the 12" mark on the tongue to the 12" mark on the blade (Figure E-3-2).*

   The number you get from this measurement (17") is the length of the run of the hip rafter overhang when the roof has a 12" overhang.

NOTE: Calculated using the first method, the hip rafter overhang was 17.04". Calculated using the second method, the hip rafter overhang was 17". A difference of .04" is not significant.

4. LAYING OUT AND CUTTING A HIP RAFTER

Once the length of the hip rafter has been determined, the layout and cutting may proceed.

At this point, you may wish to review earlier sections of this publication to refresh your memory about terms already defined when the procedure for the layout and cutting of common rafters was discussed.

The hip rafter length you determined in Section E-3 is the *theoretical length*—that is, the distance from the *center of the ridge* to the *heel plumb cut line* (Figure C-2-3). To find the *actual length*, the hip rafter must be shortened by one half of the 45° thickness of the common rafters at the end of the ridge (Figure E-4-1).

Shortening will make the top of the hip rafter fit properly between the two common rafters, which are at right angles to each other and which extend downward from the ridgeboard to the double plates at the ends and sides of the wall framing.

To lay out and cut a hip rafter, proceed as follows:

1. *Select a piece of rafter material at least 12" longer than the determined length needed (See Section E-3).*

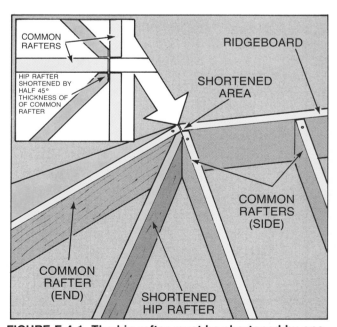

FIGURE E-4-1. The hip rafter must be shortened by one half of the 45" thickness of a common rafter.

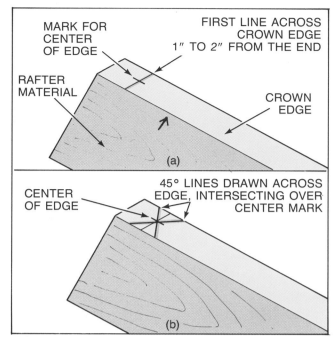

FIGURE E-4-2. To lay out a hip rafter (a) draw a line across the crown edge of the rafter material, find the center and mark it; (b) continue marking by drawing 45° lines across the edge intersecting over the center mark.

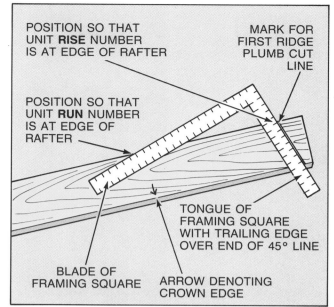

FIGURE E-4-3. Mark the first ridge plumb cut line along the tongue of the framing square when it is in the proper position.

2. *Find the crown edge, and mark it with an arrow pointing to the outside edge.*

3. *Lay the rafter material across sawhorses, with the crown edge toward you.*

4. *Using a combination square, draw a line across the crown edge of the rafter material an inch or two from the end (Figure E-4-2a).*

5. *Find the center of the edge of the rafter, and mark the location along the line you have just made (Figure E-4-2a).*

6. *With a combination square, draw two 45° lines across the edge so that they intersect over the center mark you made in step 5 (Figure E-4-2b).*

7. *Place the framing square across the face of the rafter material so that the elbow-shaped corner is pointing away from you.*

   The trailing edge of the tongue should be positioned so that the outside edge is directly over the end of the 45° line made in step 6.

8. *Position the square so that the number on the tongue corresponding to the unit* **rise** *(6″ in our example) is to your right at the upper edge of the rafter material, and so that the number on the blade corresponding to the unit* **run** *(17″ in our example) is to your left at the upper edge of the rafter material (Figure E-4-3).*

9. *Draw a line along the outside edge of the tongue, marking the ridge plumb cut line (Figure E-4-3).*

10. *Using a power hand saw tilted to full 45° angle, cut along both sides of the material at the ridge plumb cut line.*

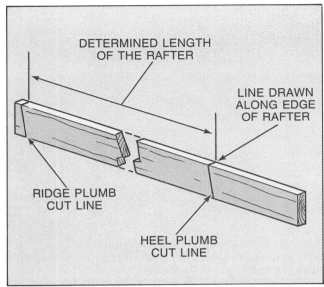

FIGURE E-4-4. Measure the determined length of the rafter from the apex of the ridge plumb cut line down the edge to identify the position of the heel plumb cut line.

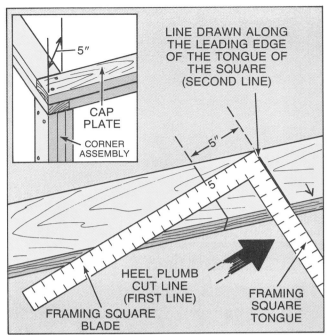

FIGURE E-4-5. Measure the diagonal width of the cap plate (inset). Then measure that distance at a right angle from the heel plumb cut line, and draw a line along the leading edge of the framing square tongue.

11. *Measure the determined length of the rafter from the apex of the ridge plumb cut line down the edge of the material to identify the position of the heel plumb cut line. Draw a line across the edge of the rafter material at the determined point (Figure E-4-4).*

    For the sample house used throughout this publication, this length has been determined to be 252″ or 21′ (see Section E-3).

12. *Using the line drawn across the edge of the rafter as a guide, repeat the marking procedures outlined in steps 5–8, and then draw a heel plumb cut line across the face of the rafter (Figure E-4-4).*

13. *Measure the width of the cap plate diagonally across the corner of the wall assembly (Figure E-4-5 inset).*

14. *Place the framing square with the blade (to the left) at right angles to the heel plumb cut line, with the number corresponding to the measurement calculated in step 13 (5″) resting on the line, and with the elbow of the framing square against the bottom edge of the rafter. Draw a line along the leading edge of the framing square tongue (Figure E-4-5).*

15. *With the framing square still in the same position, draw a third line from the heel plumb cut line (the first line) to the point where the second line (step 14) meets the bottom edge of the rafter (Figure E-4-6).*

    This is the **rafter seat cut line** of the bird's mouth for the hip rafter. Since the unit run of the hip rafter is 17″, the angles of the plumb and seat cuts are different from those on a common rafter.

16. *Draw an X in the area to be cut out for the bird's mouth (Figure E-4-6).*

17. *Use a power saw to cut out the bird's mouth using the lines you have just drawn as a guide.*

    You may wish to alter the rafter so that the alignment allows the sheathing to rest on the corners. This is accomplished by increasing the amount taken from the seat cut. Since the rafter's position drops, the procedure is known as **dropping the rafter**.

    If you intend to drop the rafter, you may wish to delay cutting until the correct amount of drop has been determined (See Section E-5).

18. *Add the determined length of the overhang by measuring down the top edge of the rafter from the heel plumb cut line. Draw a line across the edge of the rafter at this point.*

    In the calculations for our sample house, the length of this overhang has already been determined to be 17.04″ (see Section E-3).

52

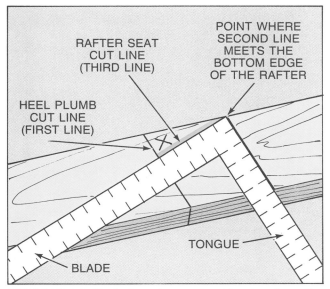

FIGURE E-4-6. Mark the rafter seat cut by drawing a line along the side of the leading edge of the framing square blade between the two parallel marks across the rafter.

19. *Using the steps already outlined in steps 5–8, draw a tail plumb cut line across the face of the rafter.*

There are two methods of trimming the end of the hip rafter for a proper fit of the **fascia board**—the horizontally fitted board nailed to the end of all rafters (Figure E-4-7).

One method involves cutting a double cheek cut to provide alignment with other rafters.

A second, and perhaps easier, procedure is to leave an extension that can be trimmed when the

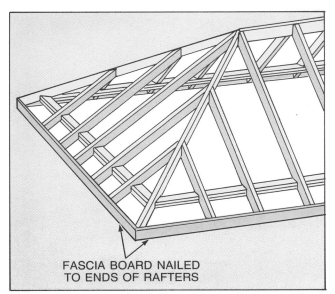

FIGURE E-4-7. The fascia board is the horizontal board nailed to the trimmed ends of the rafters.

fascia is put in place. A chalk line is snapped along the ends of all rafters from one end of the structure to the other. A sliding T-Bevel can be used to mark the plumb cut on each rafter (Figure C-2-7).

20. *Check the rafter for proper fit.*

The correct cutting of hip rafters is not an easy job. It is very possible that adjustments will have to be made and that more than one rafter may have to be cut before a satisfactory fit is achieved.

5. BACKING OR DROPPING HIP RAFTERS

Because hip rafters are installed at an angle of 45° from the common rafters, the edges of the hip rafters will be higher than those of the adjacent rafters. Thus, an alteration must be made so that the installed roof sheathing will not be higher where it covers the hip rafters than where it covers the adjacent rafters.

There are two methods of accomplishing this same objective. The first method is called *backing* or *chamfering*. Backing involves beveling the top edge of a hip rafter so that sheathing from two roof angles will align properly at the corner joint (Figure E-5-1).

Determining the correct amount to bevel off is a problem that must be worked out when using this method. Because it takes more time, backing is not as commonly used as the second method.

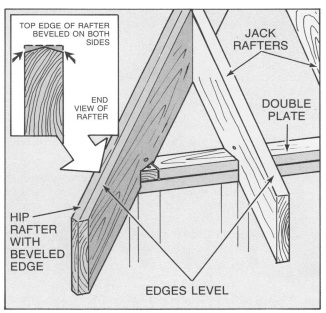

FIGURE E-5-1. Backing a hip rafter involves beveling both sides of the top edge so the edge will be the same height as the edge of the adjacent jack rafters.

53

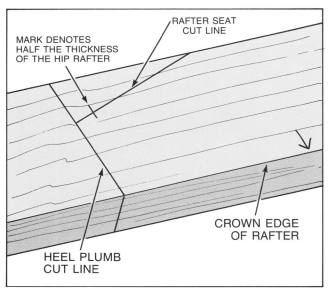

FIGURE E-5-2. Make a set forward mark ahead of the heel plumb cut line at a distance of one half the thickness of the hip rafter. Normally, this will be ¾″.

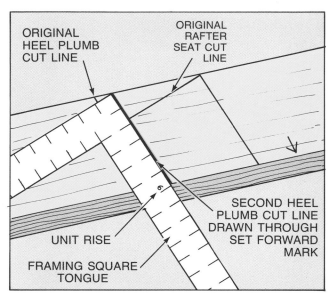

FIGURE E-5-3. Position the framing square so that the tongue passes through the set forward mark parallel to the original heel plumb cut line.

The second method—*dropping the hip*—involves enlarging the rafter seat cut by a calculated amount so that the rafter's installed position will be lower or dropped. Since the position of the rafters is lower, the corners of the hip rafter will be lowered and aligned with the tops of adjacent rafters, allowing proper alignment and fit of the installed sheathing.

To drop a hip rafter, proceed as follows:

1. *Taking a marked rafter and measuring from the heel plumb cut line along the rafter seat cut line, measure and mark a distance equal to half the thickness of the hip rafter material (Figure E-5-2).*

    This mark is called a **set forward mark** because it is set forward from the heel plumb cut line toward the forward or top part of the rafter.

    Since most rafter material is 1½″ thick (actual measurement), you will be measuring ¾″ forward along this line (Figure E-5-2).

2. *Position the framing square as follows. Position the tongue to your right, with the leading edge passing through the mark you've just made and with the number corresponding to the unit rise (6″) at the crown edge of the rafter (Figure E-5-3). Position the blade to your left, with the number corresponding to the unit run (17″) at the crown edge of the rafter.*

    Positioning the framing square in this way will ensure that the leading edge of the framing square tongue is parallel to the original heel plumb cut line.

3. *Draw a second heel plumb cut line across the leading edge of the tongue from one side of the rafter to the other (Figure E-5-3).*

4. *Beginning from the point where the rafter seat cut line and the heel plumb cut line intersect, draw a line parallel to the bottom edge of the rafter (Figure E-5-4).*

    The parallel line should continue across the second heel plumb cut line. A combination square is the best tool to use when drawing this line.

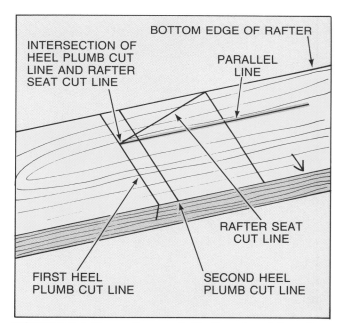

FIGURE E-5-4. Draw a line parallel to the edge of the rafter, starting from the point where the rafter seat cut and the original heel plumb cut lines intersect and continuing through the second heel plumb cut line.

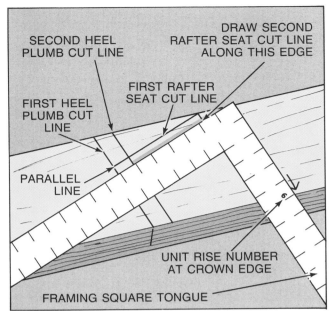

FIGURE E-5-5. Move the framing square to the right until the top edge of the blade passes through the point where the second heel plumb cut line and the line parallel to the edge cross. Draw a second rafter seat cut line along the top edge of the framing square blade.

5. *Reposition the framing square so that the tongue is to your right and the numbers corresponding to the unit rise (6") and the unit run (17") are along the crown edge of the material. Then move the square along the rafter until the point where the parallel line crosses the second heel plumb cut line is visible, with the top edge of the blade directly under that point (Figure E-5-5).*

6. *With the framing square in the same position, draw a second rafter seat cut line along the edge of the blade, parallel to the first rafter seat cut line (Figure E-5-5).*

When the bird's mouth is cut out along this second line, you will get the proper hip rafter drop for the sheathing to fit when it is attached (Figure E-5-6).

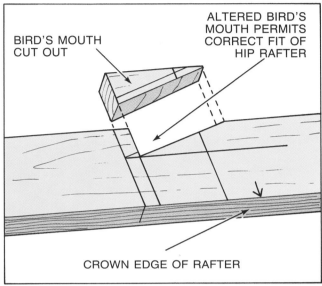

FIGURE E-5-6. Cut the modified bird's mouth out of the rafter to permit rafter to be dropped for proper sheathing fit.

6. LAYING OUT AND CUTTING JACK RAFTERS

There are two types of jack rafters. **Hip jack rafters** are used to frame the space between the hip rafter (at the top) and the double plate (at the bottom) on an *outside* corner (Figure E-6-1). **Valley jack rafters** frame the triangular area between the ridgeboard (at the top) and the valley rafter (at the bottom of two intersecting roofs) on an *inside* corner (Figure E-6-1).

These rafters, installed in pairs, should be the same distance apart as the common rafters on the gable section of the roof. Where the ends of these rafters meet a hip or valley rafter, a cheek or side cut must be made, with an opposite cut made on the opposite rafter.

Hip jack rafters, like common rafters, overhang the outside wall, but valley jack rafters have no overhang since their bottoms rest on the valley rafter. Except for this difference, the two types are alike and can be measured, cut, and assembled in the same way.

Since jack rafters fill in a triangle formed by the last common rafter and the hip or valley rafter, they will vary in length. The closer the jack rafters get to the bottom of the hip rafter or the top of the valley rafter, the shorter they will be.

The consistent distance between the rafters is known as the *common length difference.* When the layout is started from the longest hip or valley jack rafter nearest

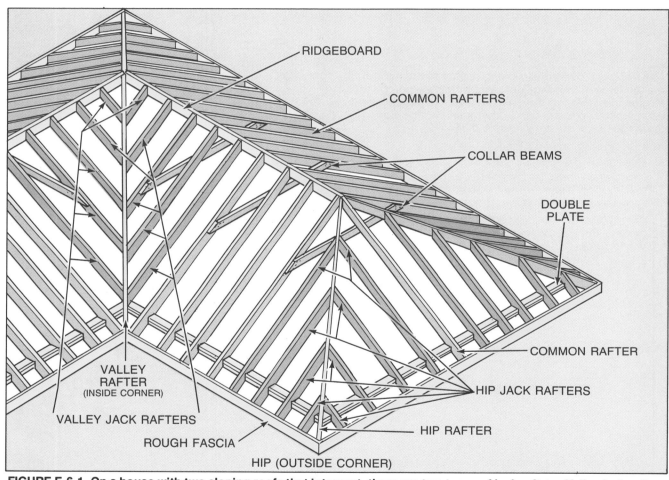

FIGURE E-6-1. On a house with two sloping roofs that intersect, there are two types of jack rafters. Valley jack rafters frame the space between the ridgeboard at the top and the valley rafter at the bottom and are always found on inside corners. Hip jack rafters frame the space between the hip rafter at the top and the double plate at the bottom and are always located on the outside corners.

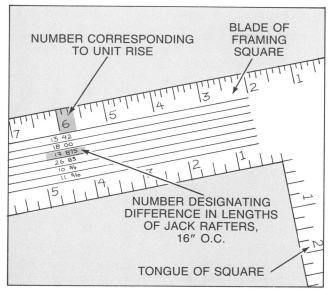

FIGURE E-6-2. Look along the top edge of the framing square blade to locate the number that corresponds to the unit rise. Look at the third line below that number to find the number designating the difference in the length of jack rafters spaced 16" O.C.

the last common rafter, the length of the remaining rafters can be determined by subtracting the common length difference from each successive rafter.

Layout and cutting of jack rafters is discussed under two headings:

a. Determining Jack Rafter Lengths
b. Laying Out and Cutting Jack Rafters

a. Determining Jack Rafter Lengths

The procedure described here assumes that you are beginning the layout from a common rafter at the end of the ridgeboard. This is the method of construction discussed earlier.

The example used is the house described in previous examples, which has a roof unit rise of 6" and a span of 28'. The length of the common rafter at the end of the ridge was determined to be 15'8" in Section B-3. Rafters are spaced 16" O.C.

To determine jack rafter lengths, proceed as follows:

1. *Find the number that corresponds to the unit rise (6")
along the top edge of the blade of the framing square*
(Figure E-6-2).

2. *Look directly below that number (6") to the third line
on the framing square where the difference in length
of jack rafters spaced 16" O.C. may be found.*

   In this case, the number is 17.875" or 1'5.875"
(Figure E-6-2).

3. *Convert the decimal (.875) to a fraction of an inch
by using the decimal equivalents chart in Table II of
this book.*

   A look at the chart shows the decimal .875" can be converted to $\frac{7}{8}$". Thus, the common length difference is 1'5$\frac{7}{8}$".

4. *To determine the length of the first pair of jack rafters,
subtract the common length difference shown on the
rafter table (17.875" or 1'5$\frac{7}{8}$") from the known length
of the common rafters (15'8") (Figure E-6-3).*

   First, subtract the feet from the feet:

$$\begin{array}{r} 15' \\ -1' \\ \hline 14' \end{array}$$

   Next, subtract the inches from the inches:

$$\begin{array}{r} 8'' \\ -5\frac{7}{8}'' \\ \hline \end{array} = \begin{array}{r} 7\frac{8}{8}'' \\ -5\frac{7}{8}'' \\ \hline 2\frac{1}{8}'' \end{array}$$

Thus, the first pair of jack rafters should be 14'2$\frac{1}{8}$" in length.

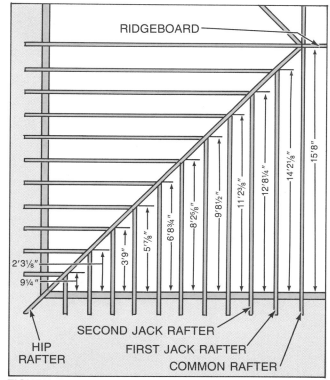

FIGURE E-6-3. Each pair of jack rafters (beginning with the longest next to the ridgeboard) is shorter than the adjacent pair by a consistent amount, known as the common length difference.

5. *To find the length of the second pair of jack rafters, subtract the common length difference (1'5⅞") from the length of the first pair of jack rafters (14'2⅛") (Figure E-6-3).*

You cannot subtract 5⅞" from 2⅛", so first borrow 1' (12") from the 14':

$$14'2\tfrac{1}{8}'' = 13'14\tfrac{1}{8}''$$

Next subtract the feet from the feet:

$$
\begin{array}{r}
13'\\
-\ 1'\\
\hline
12'
\end{array}
$$

Next, subtract the inches from the inches:

$$
\begin{array}{r}
14\tfrac{1}{8}''\\
-5\tfrac{7}{8}''\\
\hline
\end{array}
\quad = \quad
\begin{array}{r}
13\tfrac{9}{8}''\\
-5\tfrac{7}{8}''\\
\hline
8\tfrac{2}{8}''\ \text{or}\ 8\tfrac{1}{4}''
\end{array}
$$

Thus, the second pair of jack rafters should be 12'8¼" in length.

6. *To find the length of the third pair of jack rafters, subtract the common length difference (1'5⅞") from the length of the second pair of jack rafters (12'8¼") (Figure E-6-3).*

First, subtract the feet from the feet:

$$
\begin{array}{r}
12'\\
-\ 1'\\
\hline
11'
\end{array}
$$

Next, subtract the inches from the inches:

$$
\begin{array}{r}
8\tfrac{1}{4}'' = 8\tfrac{2}{8}'' = 7\tfrac{10}{8}''\\
-5\ \tfrac{7}{8}''\\
\hline
2\ \tfrac{3}{8}''
\end{array}
$$

Thus, the third pair of jack rafters should be 11'2⅜" in length.

7. *Continue subtracting the common length difference (1'5⅞") from the length of each preceding pair of rafters until the last rafter is within 16" of the end of the overhang of the hip rafter.*

After making the necessary calculations, you will find that the lengths of each pair of jack rafters will be as shown in Figure E-6-3, which is a plan view of one corner of the hip roof you are constructing.

b. Laying Out and Cutting Jack Rafters

Once the lengths of the jack rafters have been determined, the layout and cutting can begin. Remember that the determined length does not include the overhang that must be added to each jack rafter. Something else to keep in mind as you get ready to mark and cut these rafters is the importance of accurate measuring and cutting to ensure a good tight fit.

Since our sample house has a simple hip roof with matching hip areas on both ends, you would need to mark and cut *four times* as many jack rafters (two sets at each of the four corners) as were calculated earlier in this discussion. Obviously, if calculations are correct, the process can be speeded up by marking all needed rafters using the master sets you cut first.

Since you already know the length of all jack rafters, select lumber for the longest rafter to begin the marking process. Remember to add enough length for the overhang. In our sample house, the overhang is 12".

To lay out and cut the jack rafters, proceed as follows:

1. *Use a combination square to draw a squared line across the top of the rafter's crown edge (Figure E-6-4).*

This line should be drawn within several inches of the end of the board.

2. *Mark the center of the rafter edge along the line you've just drawn (Figure E-6-4).*

If you are using 2"-thick (nominal measure) lumber, the actual width is 1½", so the center will be ¾" from the edge.

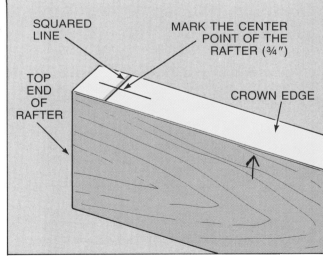

FIGURE E-6-4. Square a line across the edge of the rafter, and mark the center of the edge along that line.

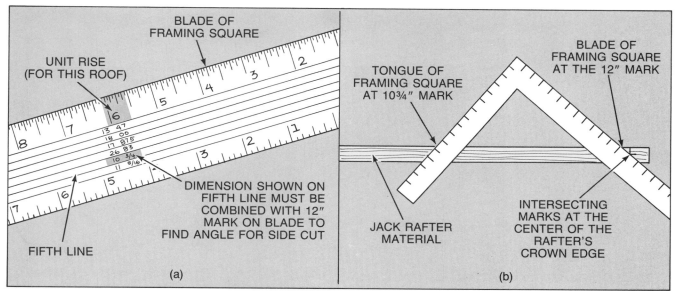

FIGURE E-6-5a. The number (10¾″) found on the fifth line of the framing square blade under the number designating the unit rise (6″ in this example) is needed to find the angle of the side cut.

FIGURE E-6-5b. Place the framing square *tongue* across the edge of the rafter material at the 10¾″ mark, and place the framing square *blade* at the 12″ mark with the edge of the tail running through the intersecting marks at the center of the rafter's crown edge.

3. *Find the number corresponding to the unit rise (6″) on your framing square blade, and then locate the dimension listed on the fifth line below that unit rise mark (Figure E-6-5a).*

   The dimension in this case is 10¾″.

4. *Position the framing square across the edge of the rafter material so that the blade is to your right, the 12″ mark is at the top edge of the lumber, and the blade edge runs through the middle of the mark you made in step 2 (Figure E-6-5b).*

   The 12″ mark is used since we are discussing and measuring rise per foot (12″) of run.

5. *Position the tongue leg of the framing square to your left, with the dimension you identified in step 3 (10¾″) aligned with the top edge of the lumber (Figure E-6-5b).*

6. *Mark a line along the edge of the blade (Figure E-6-6).*

   This line marks the angle for the side cut.

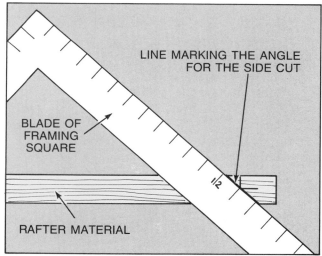

FIGURE E-6-6. Draw a line along the blade edge that passes through the center mark near the end of the rafter. This line marks the angle for the side cut.

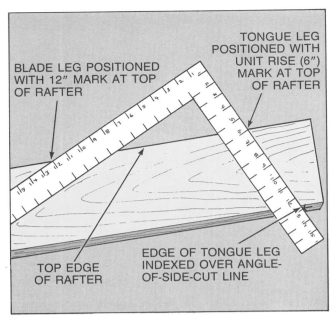

BLADE LEG POSITIONED WITH 12″ MARK AT TOP OF RAFTER

TONGUE LEG POSITIONED WITH UNIT RISE (6″) MARK AT TOP OF RAFTER

TOP EDGE OF RAFTER

EDGE OF TONGUE LEG INDEXED OVER ANGLE-OF-SIDE-CUT LINE

FIGURE E-6-7. To mark the line for the side cut, position the framing square across the rafter so that the blade leg is aligned with the top of the rafter at the 12″ mark and the tongue leg at the 6″ (unit rise) mark. The trailing leg of the tongue must meet the end of the line made across the edge previously to mark the angle for the side cut.

7. *Turn the rafter material on its side, with the marked edge toward you (Figure E-6-7).*

8. *Lay the framing square across the rafter material. Position the tongue leg to the right so that the number corresponding to the unit rise (6″) is at the top edge (Figure E-6-7).*

9. *Pivot the blade leg of the framing square so the 12″ mark is flush with the top edge (Figure E-6-7).*

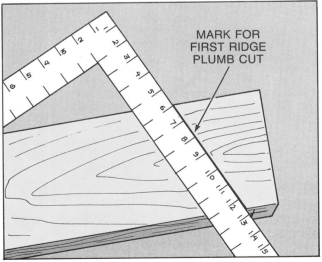

MARK FOR FIRST RIDGE PLUMB CUT

FIGURE E-6-8. Mark the first ridge plumb cut line (side cut) along the edge of the tongue of the framing square.

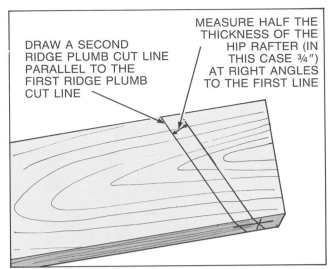

DRAW A SECOND RIDGE PLUMB CUT LINE PARALLEL TO THE FIRST RIDGE PLUMB CUT LINE

MEASURE HALF THE THICKNESS OF THE HIP RAFTER (IN THIS CASE ¾″) AT RIGHT ANGLES TO THE FIRST LINE

FIGURE E-6-9. Shorten the jack rafter by marking a line ¾″ away from and parallel to the first ridge plumb cut line.

10. *Mark the ridge plumb cut by drawing a line along the tongue edge (Figure E-6-8).*

    This is the *first* ridge plumb cut line.

11. *At right angles to the first ridge plumb cut line, measure a distance equal to one half the thickness of the hip rafter, and make another line parallel to the first one (Figure E-6-9).*

    This is the *second* ridge plumb cut line, which shortens the jack rafter by half the thickness of the hip rafter. The shortening must be done here for the same reason that the common rafters were shortened. See Section C-2 for more information.

12. *Measure and mark the determined body length of the jack rafter. Start from the line drawn in step 1 and measure down the edge of the rafter (Figure E-6-10).*

    The body length of the longest jack rafter was determined earlier (Section 6a) to be 14′2⅛″.

13. *Use a combination square to draw a line across the edge through this mark.*

14. *Using procedures already outlined in steps 7–10, draw a heel plumb cut line across the face of the rafter (Figure E-6-10).*

15. *Lay out the bird's mouth by marking the rafter seat cut line as outlined in Section C-2 (Figure E-6-10).*

16. *Add the distance for the rafter overhang by measuring from the heel plumb cut line down the edge of the rafter (Figure E-6-10).*

    As previously discussed, the overhang is 12″. You'll need to add more than 12″ to allow for the tail plumb cut. You may wish to wait and trim any excess off later, as discussed earlier in Section C-2.

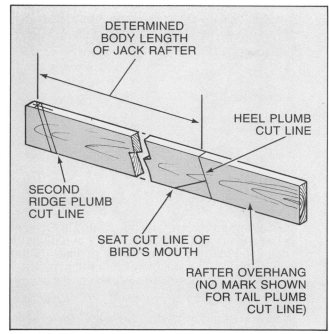

FIGURE E-6-10. Starting from the first mark made on the rafter edge, measure and mark the determined body length of the jack rafter. This mark indicates the position of the heel plumb cut line. The rafter overhang will be measured from this line.

7. ERECTING A HIP ROOF FRAME

Erecting the middle section of a hip roof is much like erecting a gable roof frame.

Earlier, in Section E-2, determining the length of the ridgeboard for a hip roof was discussed. You will recall that there are *theoretical* and *actual* ridgeboard lengths. The *actual* length includes half the thickness of the common rafter at each end, which is necessary if the end hip has a common rafter (Figures E-2-1 and E-2-2). The roof in our example has such a common rafter.

Safety is most important when assembly is underway. Care should be taken in regard to leaning or walking on rafters that have not been stabilized and working over ceiling joists and open areas. A temporary platform of boards, scaffolding, or sheathing should be provided for workers to stand upon during the erection process.

To erect a hip roof frame, proceed as follows:

1. *Use the procedure outlined in Section C-5 to attach the ridgeboard to a pair of common rafters at each end* (Figure E-7-1).

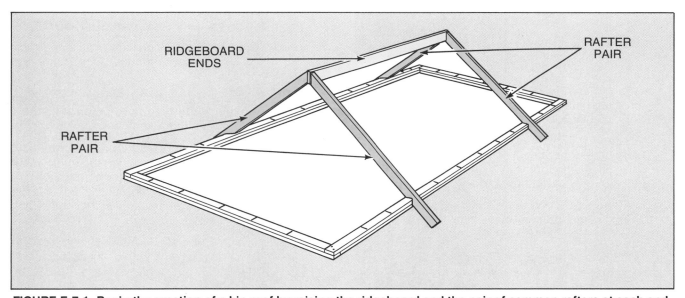

FIGURE E-7-1. Begin the erection of a hip roof by raising the ridgeboard and the pair of common rafters at each end.

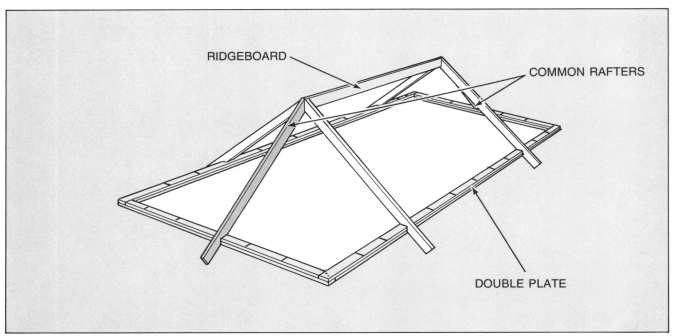

FIGURE E-7-2. Position and nail in place the common rafters that go from the ends of the ridgeboard down to the double plate at each end of the structure.

2. *Position and nail a single common rafter in place at each end of the ridgeboard with 16d nails (Figure E-7-2).*

3. *Place the hip rafters in position in each of the four corners, and (with 16d nails) nail them to the double plate and to the end of the ridgeboard (Figure E-7-3).*

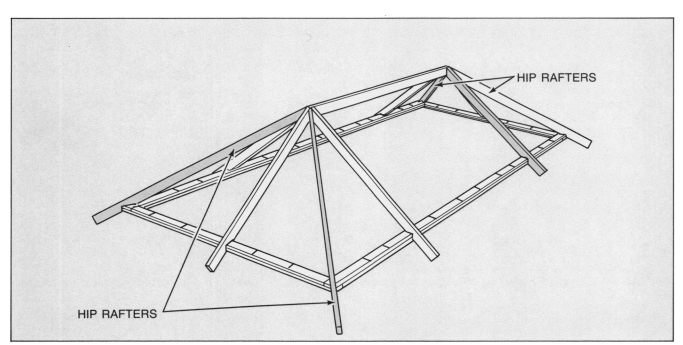

FIGURE E-7-3. Place the hip rafters in position at each corner of the house.

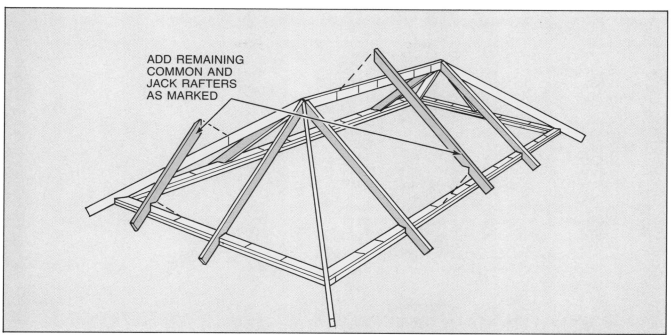

FIGURE E-7-4. Complete the framing by positioning and installing the remaining common and jack rafters on all sides.

4. *Install the jack rafters in pairs by nailing each rafter first to the marked double plate and then to the hip rafter (Figure E-7-4).*

5. *Position and install the remaining common rafters along the ridgeboard using 16d nails (Figue E-7-4).*

6. *Measure, cut, and install collar beams as described earlier in Section C-6.*

STUDY QUESTIONS

1. To calculate the theoretical length of the ridgeboard for a hip roof, what value do you subtract from the length of the house (in feet)?

2. To calculate the actual length of the ridgeboard, you increase the theoretical length by one half the thickness of what?

3. Why must a hip rafter travel longer than a common rafter to reach a ridgeboard of the same height?

4. Where on the framing square blade do you look to find the length in inches of a hip rafter per foot of run?

5. To calculate the determined length of a hip rafter (in inches), you multiply the length in inches per foot of run by what value?

6. What distance must a hip rafter overhang extend beyond the double plate for every 1″ a common rafter extends?

7. How many feet are there in 132″ ?

8. When laying out a hip rafter, you first use a combination square to draw a squared line with two 45° lines across it. Where on the rafter material do you draw these lines?

9. What does *dropping the rafter* mean?

10. What purpose does dropping the rafter serve?

11. What mark is the SET FORWARD MARK set forward from?

12. How much is the SET FORWARD MARK set forward?

13. On an outside corner, hip jack rafters frame the space between the hip rafter (at the top) and what (at the bottom)?

14. On an inside corner, valley jack rafters frame the triangular area between the valley rafter (at the bottom of two intersecting roofs) and what (at the top)?

15. Where on the framing square blade do you look to find the difference in length of jack rafters spaced 16″ O.C.?

16. Subtract 5⅞″ from 13′2⅜″.

17. Where on the framing square blade do you locate the dimension to be used (on the tongue) with 12″ (on the blade) to mark the angle for the side cut on a jack rafter?

18. When installing jack rafters, one end is nailed to the hip rafter and one end is nailed to the double plate. Which end should be nailed first?

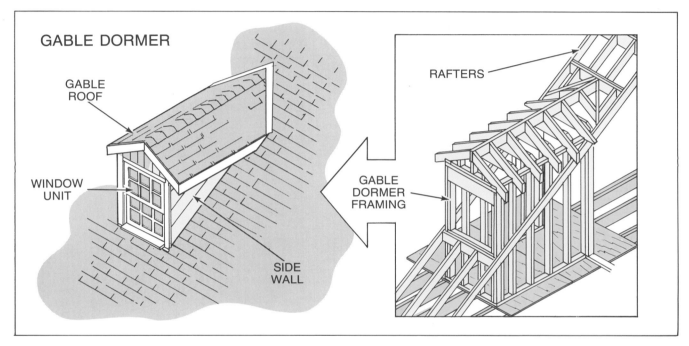

FIGURE F-1. A gable dormer has a gable roof and generally contains a window. In this example, the dormer is framed inside the opening, with the base built on top of the ceiling/floor framing (inset).

A **dormer** is a framework that projects upward through the roof, containing a window or vent to add ventilation, light, or space. Dormers also change the appearance of a house and are most commonly found on houses with steep roofs. There are two basic types of dormers: gable and shed.

Gable dormers (also known as **doghouse dormers**), generally used on the front side of homes, normally are rather narrow, have side walls, and contain a window (Figure F-1). These dormers usually are framed on top of the *roof framing* in an opening provided (Figure F-2). Another method of construction allows the dormer to be built inside of an opening made in the roof, with the base construction resting on the top of the *ceiling/floor framing* (Figure F-1).

Shed-type dormers are most often used on the back of homes with a steep pitched roof. They may be a few feet wide or extend the length of the roof (Figure F-3). The primary purpose of shed-type dormers is to provide additional space, light, and ventilation in the room or rooms underneath the roof.

Framing dormers is discussed under the following headings:

1. Framing a Roof Opening for a Dormer
2. Framing a Gable Dormer with Side Walls
3. Framing a Shed-type Dormer with Side Walls

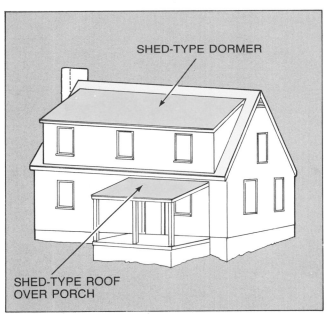

FIGURE F-2. Some dormers are framed on top of doubled rafters on either side of the dormer's base.

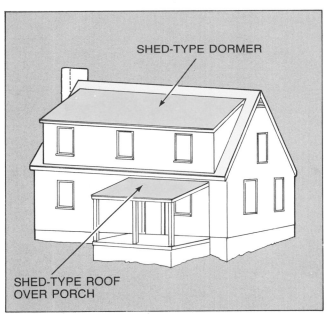

FIGURE F-3. Shed-type dormers may extend across the length of a roof to provide additional space, light, and ventilation.

1. FRAMING A ROOF OPENING FOR A DORMER

Dormers are built through openings in the roof. These openings are framed in a manner that is similar to the framing of openings for stairways and scuttles in a floor or ceiling frame.

If the dormer is to be built with the framing resting on top of the rafters, the rafters on either side of the opening must be doubled. All headers at the top and bottom of an opening should also be doubled (Figure F-1-1).

The headers at the top of the opening are usually set at a right angle to the slope of the roof (Figure F-1-1). Since most dormers have windows, the header at the bottom of the opening is set plumb so that the top of the doubled header will act as a rough sill for the window unit.

Some carpenters prefer to install all rafters in their designated position (16″ or 24″ O.C.) before making provision for any opening in the roof. This approach may be easier, since all common rafters are generally cut from a pattern rafter and can quickly be cut and put into position.

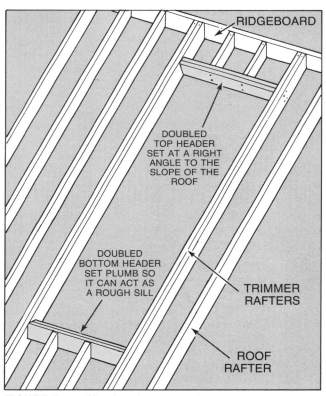

FIGURE F-1-1. Headers in an opening in the roof framing should be doubled. The top header is set at a right angle to the slope of the roof, whereas the bottom header is set plumb to accommodate a window unit.

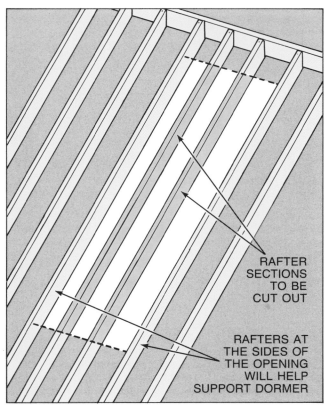

RAFTER
SECTIONS
TO BE
CUT OUT

RAFTERS AT
THE SIDES OF
THE OPENING
WILL HELP
SUPPORT DORMER

FIGURE F-1-2. When openings are made in a roof frame after full rafters have been installed, portions of the rafters have to be cut and discarded.

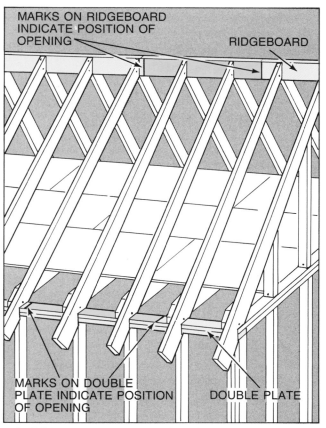

MARKS ON RIDGEBOARD
INDICATE POSITION OF
OPENING

RIDGEBOARD

MARKS ON DOUBLE
PLATE INDICATE POSITION
OF OPENING

DOUBLE PLATE

FIGURE F-1-3. Mark the ridgeboard and double plate for the position of the planned opening.

A drawback to this procedure is the material wasted when the excess lumber is cut from the opening area (Figure F-1-2). Waste can be minimized by using these short pieces for braces and cripple rafters elsewhere in the building project.

An alternate method for framing an opening involves leaving rafters out in those areas where openings will occur. Rafters will still be installed at their normal 16″ or 24″O.C. intervals, but shorter cripple rafters will need to be cut and installed above and below the headers. The cripple rafters will be placed in the position that full rafters would normally occupy (16″ or 24″ O.C.). To save material and speed construction, this is the preferred method when a longer opening (over 10′) will be needed.

When framing an opening using either method, the roof frame should be checked for plumb and straightened if necessary. After headers are installed, straightening is more difficult.

To frame a roof opening for a dormer, proceed as follows:

1. *Using the building plans, determine the length and width of the opening needed for the dormer.*

2. *Lay out the location of the opening on the ridgeboard and the double plate* (Figure F-1-3).

   NOTE: The procedure outlined assumes that all rafters have been installed at their regular intervals.

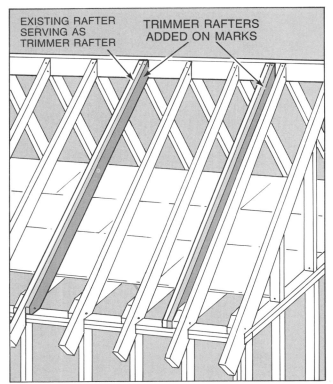

FIGURE F-1-4. Add trimmer rafters where indicated by the marks on the ridgeboard and double plate.

3. *Install doubled trimmer rafter(s) as needed according to the marks on the ridgeboard and double plate* (Figure F-1-4).

   An existing rafter in its standard position can serve as a trimmer rafter. However, rarely will all common rafters be positioned where trimmers are needed, and thus, adding trimmers will be necessary. A trimmer rafter does not have to have a tail or overhang, since it is positioned next to a complete rafter.

4. *Using the rafters nearest to the outsides of the planned opening, measure and mark the top and bottom of the opening* (Figure F-1-5).

   First measure down from the ridgeboard to the top of the opening, and mark that location on the rafter. Then, measure the length of the opening down the rafter from the first mark, and mark this second location on the rafter. Repeat this procedure on the rafter on the other side of the opening. Be sure to allow for the top and bottom headers—3″ at the top of the opening and 3″ at the bottom.

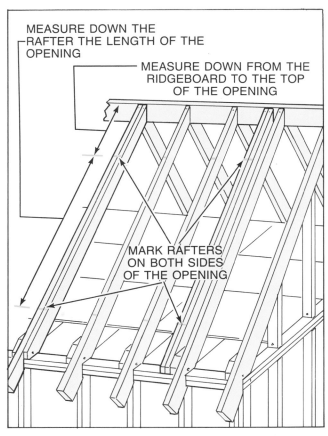

FIGURE F-1-5. Measure and mark the rafters with lines to indicate the top and bottom of the opening.

5. *Repeat this marking procedure for all openings of the same size across the length of the roof.*

   You should double-check these marks for accuracy before proceeding to the next step.

6. *With a chalk line, mark a line across the rafters from the outside of the first dormer opening to the outside of the last dormer opening.*

7. *Using a sliding T-bevel, mark a plumb cut on each rafter at the bottom of the opening, and mark a right angle on each rafter at the top of the opening* (Figure F-1-6).

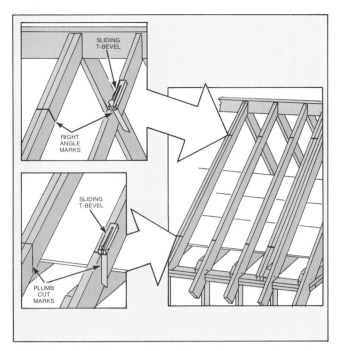

FIGURE F-1-6. Use a sliding T-bevel to mark the rafters in the area of the opening.

8. *Using the lines made in steps 6 and 7, cut the rafters inside the proposed opening.*

9. *Measure the distance between the outside rafters at the top and bottom of each opening, and cut and install headers (Figure F-1-7).*

   Nail through the outside of the trimmer rafters into the ends of the headers with 16d nails. Add cripple rafters above the top header and below the bottom header, and nail through the header into the ends of the cripple rafters with 16d nails (Figure F-1-7).

10. *Cut second headers and install them on the inside of the first headers—top and bottom—using 16d nails to secure them in place (Figure F-1-8).*

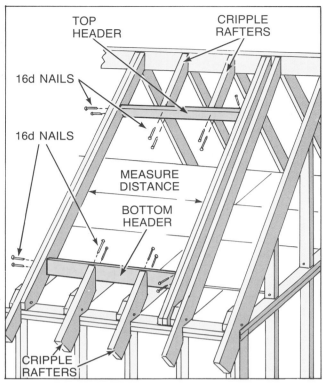

FIGURE F-1-7. After the rafters are cut out of the opening, a header should be nailed in place at the top and bottom of the opening. Although headers are usually nailed to the trimmer rafters with the nails going through the trimmer and into the header, some headers will need to be toenailed to the rafter (as shown on the right above) because of space constraints.

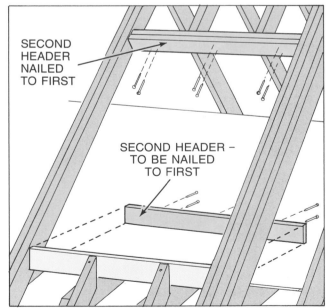

FIGURE F-1-8. Nail a second header to the first header at the top and bottom of the opening.

2. FRAMING A GABLE DORMER WITH SIDE WALLS

To frame a gable dormer with side walls, proceed as follows. The procedure outlined assumes that you have already framed an opening in the roof frame as discussed earlier.

1. *Using the drawing on the plans, determine the total height of the dormer wall and the height of the corner posts* (Figure F-2-1).

2. *Construct corner post assemblies in the length needed according to your calculations.*

   Posts should be somewhat longer than the exact length needed to allow for trimming. You may wish to review the information on building corner posts in Section D of *Wall Framing* (AAVIM, 1989).

3. *Using a sliding T-bevel adjusted to match the angle of the rafters, mark the bottom of the post assembly.*

4. *From the long side of the bevel, measure the exact length needed for the corner post and trim off the excess.*

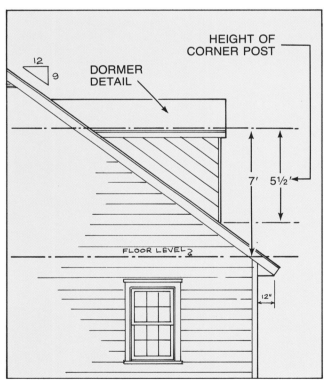

FIGURE F-2-1. Dormer details on house plans can be used to determine the height of corner posts.

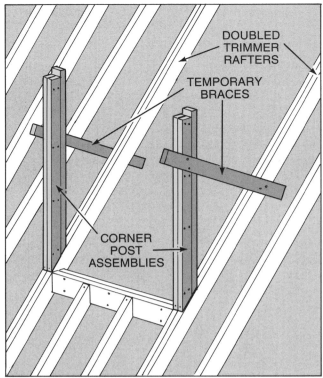

FIGURE F-2-2. Nail the corner post assemblies to the top of the doubled trimmer rafters. Temporary braces may have to be installed to maintain the plumb of corner posts.

5. *Nail the bottom of the post assemblies to the top of the rafter with 16d nails* (Figure F-2-2).

   As you nail the posts in place, be sure to check for plumb. You may need to add temporary braces until the assembly can be steadied with the addition of a top plate and cap plate.

6. *Measure the distance between the outside edges of the doubled trimmer rafters on each side of the dormer opening to determine the total width of the top plate.*

   This measurement should always be made at the *bottom* of the corner post, never at the top. The corner posts may not be absolutely plumb, and a measurement made at the top may not be accurate.

7. *Cut the top plate, and cut a cap plate 7" shorter than the top plate* (Figure F-2-3).

   The top plate is nailed to the tops of the posts on either side of the dormer. The cap plate is centered on the top plate to allow 3½" on either side for the fastening of the rafter plate. After nailing the top plate onto the ends of the posts, check to make sure the posts are still plumb, and make any necessary adjustments.

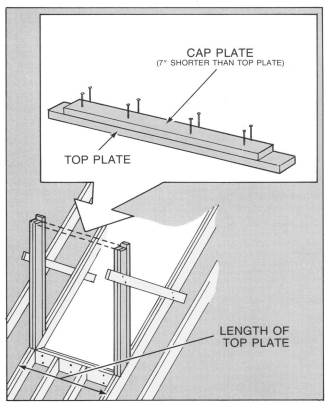

FIGURE F-2-3. Measure the distance between the outside edges of the doubled trimmer rafters to find the length of the top plate. The cap plate should be 7″ shorter than the top plate to allow room for a dormer rafter plate on either side (inset).

8. *Measure the distance from the front side of a post to the edge of the trimmer rafters to determine the length of the rafter plates. Cut the rafter plates, and bevel the ends to match the angle of the trimmer rafters (Figure F-2-4).*

9. *Nail the front portion of the rafter plate to the top of the top plate with 16d nails; toenail the beveled portion to the top of the trimmer rafters (Figure F-2-4).*

   This plate must be level—check it with a spirit level.

10. *Mark the position of the dormer studs 16″ O.C. on the rafter plate and (with the help of a plumb bob or a 4′ level) on the doubled trimmer rafters.*

    NOTE: Depending upon the configuration of the opening needed for the window unit, additional cripple studs may be needed at the top and bottom of the front assembly. Remember that the rough opening should be 2″ wider and 4″ taller than the window sash you plan to use. See Section C of *Wall Framing* (AAVIM, 1989) for additional information.

11. *Cut the dormer studs to length, and secure them in place with 16d nails.*

    Nail through the rafter plate into the top end of the studs. Toenail the base of each stud to the doubled trimmer rafters.

12. *Measure across the upper header, and make a mark at the center. To indicate the position of the gable ridgeboard, measure and mark ¾″ on either side of the center mark.*

13. *Using your house plans, determine the length of the gable ridgeboard. Select a piece of lumber (generally a 2″ × 4″ or 2″ × 6″) that is 8″ to 10″ longer to compensate for any loss when angle cuts are made.*

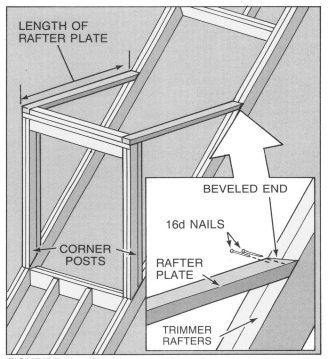

FIGURE F-2-4. The dormer rafter plates should be nailed to the tops of the corner posts and the trimmer rafters with 16d nails (inset).

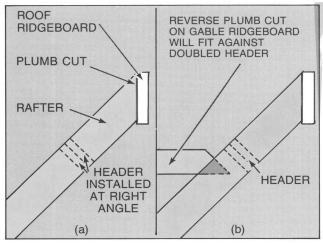

FIGURE F-2-5. (a) The plumb cut on a rafter is vertical when installed against the ridgeboard. (b) A reverse plumb cut is a plumb cut turned upside down to fit flush against a doubled header installed at a right angle.

14. *Make a reverse plumb cut on one end of the gable ridgeboard.*

    Information on making plumb cuts was discussed earlier in this publication. A rafter **plumb cut** is designed so that the cut on the rafter is *vertical* when that piece is in position in the roof structure (Figure F-2-5a). A **reverse plumb cut** is a plumb cut turned upside down so that the installed apex of the cut angle is at the *bottom* instead of the top (Figure F-2-5b).

15. *Mark the location of the rafters 16" O.C. on the gable ridgeboard.*

16. *Using the information presented in Section C of this publication, determine the length of the gable end rafters, and mark and cut the number of dormer rafters needed.*

    The rafters for the dormer roof will be cut like the rafters for the main roof. Although dormer rafters are much shorter in length, they will have the same unit rise and run as do the rafters on the roof of the house. Dormers with a pitch of 8/12 or higher are aesthetically more pleasing.

    One other possible difference involves the cut at the base of dormer rafters. If the roof of the dormer is to fit flush with the outside wall of the dormer, a **seat cut** will be needed (Figure F-2-6a). If an overhang is desired, a **bird's mouth cut** may be needed to provide the overhang framing base. The overhang on a dormer (if any) should be much less than that of the main roof (Figure F-2-6b).

17. *Nail the end rafters to the marked gable ridgeboard.*

18. *Install the ridgeboard and end gable assembly by nailing the bottoms of the gable end rafters to the dormer rafter plate with 16d nails. Attach the ridgeboard to the doubled header with 16d nails.*

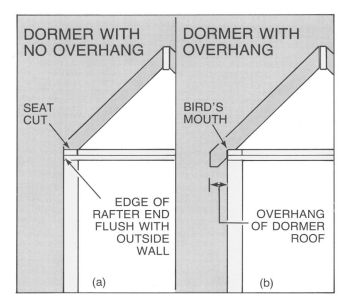

FIGURE F-2-6. The bottom ends of the rafter must be cut to provide (a) no roof overhang or (b) a small overhang.

19. *Determine the length of the valley rafters.*

    This distance is usually measured from the center of the gable ridgeboard and doubled header diagonally down to the point where the dormer rafter plate and the trimmer rafters meet (Figure F-2-7). The cut at the top of the valley rafter will normally be a **double side cut**, whereas the cut at the bottom will be a **single side cut**. These cuts will be necessary for a good tight fit of all component pieces.

20. *Mark and cut the valley rafters.*

21. *Nail the valley rafters in place using 16d nails.*

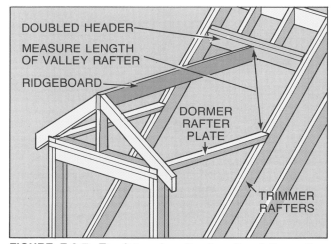

FIGURE F-2-7. To determine the length of the valley rafters, measure from the top of the intersection of the ridgeboard and doubled header to the point where the dormer rafter plate meets the trimmer rafters.

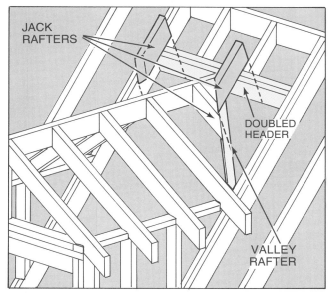

FIGURE F-2-8. Measure, cut, and install the jack rafters between the valley rafters and the doubled header.

22. *Install the remaining dormer rafters in pairs.*

23. *Cut the jack rafters, and nail them into place between the valley rafter and the doubled header (Figure F-2-8).*

3. FRAMING A SHED-TYPE DORMER WITH SIDE WALLS

Although shed-type dormers may be as small as most gable dormers, the majority are much larger. The most common shed-type dormer is at least as wide as the width required for a bathroom in a so-called **story-and-a-half house**. This type of house has living space under the roof, which means that part of the ceilings in this second-floor area are sloped in the same way as the roof rafters.

The roof of the shed-type dormer extends from the main roof at a flatter angle than the main roof, allowing for increased headroom and living space. More often than not, the shed-type dormer will extend across the biggest part of the roof—generally at the back of the house.

The steps outlined in this section are for construction of a larger shed-type dormer. Proceed as follows:

1. *Determine the size of opening needed using the building plans.*

2. *Frame the opening as outlined in the earlier section on framing a roof opening.*

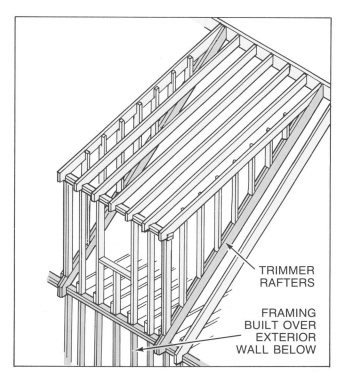

FIGURE F-3-1. Framing for larger dormers is built on trimmer rafters and over the exterior wall of the framing below.

3. *If the front wall of the dormer does not extend over the exterior wall of the first floor below, frame the front section as described in the steps in Section F-2.*

   In the event that the front wall is directly over the exterior wall below, framing should be built on doubled trimmer rafters and over the ceiling/floor framing below (Figure F-3-1).*

4. *Measure, lay out, and cut the rafters for the shed-type dormer's common rafters.*

   Procedures for doing so are covered in Section G.

5. *Mark the positions of the shed rafters on the double plate on the front wall of the dormer and on the ridgeboard (Figure F-3-2).*

6. *Place the precut rafters in position, and nail them to the double plate and the ridgeboard with 16d nails.*

7. *Mark the locations of the side wall studs 16″ O.C. on the dormer rafter plate and the doubled trimmer rafters of the main roof.*

   A plumb bob will help you determine the correct position of the base of the studs.

8. *Cut studs to length.*

   The lower ends of the studs will have to be beveled to match the angle of the doubled trimmer rafters. Notch the upper ends of the studs as outlined in Section D-2.

73

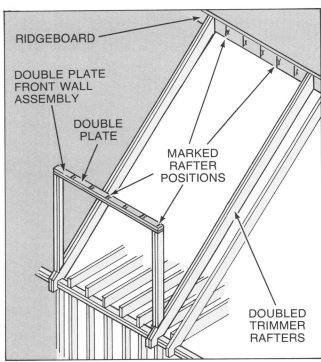

FIGURE F-3-2. Mark the positions for the dormer rafters on the ridgeboard and the double plate on the front wall assembly.

8. *Cut studs to length.*

The lower ends of the studs will have to be beveled to match the angle of the doubled trimmer rafters. Notch the upper ends of the studs as outlined in Section D-2.

STUDY QUESTIONS

1. **True or False**. Dormers are most often found on flatter roofs.

2. Dormers may be framed on top of the roof framing. What else might the dormer base construction rest upon?

3. There are gable dormers and shed-type dormers. Which type is usually found on the front of a house?

4. Dormers are designed to provide additional space and/or light. What else can they provide?

5. Why is the header at the bottom of a gable dormer opening set plumb?

6. Installing all rafters before cutting the dormer opening is easier. What is the drawback to this approach?

7. Shorter rafters installed above and below the dormer headers are called what?

8. In measuring and marking the top and bottom of the dormer opening, how many inches should be allowed for the headers?

9. **True or False**. To determine the width of the top plate, you measure between the outside edges of the tops of the corner posts.

10. Why is the cap plate cut 7″ shorter than the top plate?

11. Dormer studs are nailed at the top end and toe-nailed at the bottom end. To what framing members are they secured at each end?

12. What kind of cut must be made on one end of a gable ridgeboard so that it fits snugly against the top header?

13. What kind of cut must be made on the bottom end of gable rafters if the dormer roof is to fit flush with the outside wall?

14. The distance from the center of the ridge and doubled header diagonally down to the point where the dormer rafter plate and trimmer rafters meet is equal to the length of what framing member?

15. Is the roof of a shed-type dormer at a flatter or steeper angle than the main roof?

16. The lower end of the side wall studs for a shed-type dormer must be beveled. What angle must that bevel match?

17. After marking stud positions on the shed-type dormer's rafter plate, what tool can you use to help you locate stud positions on the doubled trimmer rafters?

G.

Laying Out, Cutting & Installing Shed-type Roof Rafters

A shed-type roof is an easier roof to construct because it only has one slope (Figure G-1). Some houses have shed-type roofs as their main roof, but they are more commonly found on outbuildings. Shed-type roofs are also used as coverings for porches attached to houses with gable and hip roofs.

Most shed-type roofs span areas that can be covered with a single length of lumber (Figure G-2a). When there is an exception to this, the ends of the rafters must overlap over a load-bearing wall (Figure G-2b).

Laying out, cutting, and installing shed-type roofs is discussed under the following headings:

1. Determining the Length of a Common Rafter for a Shed-type Roof
2. Laying Out a Pattern Shed-type Rafter
3. Installing Shed-type Rafters

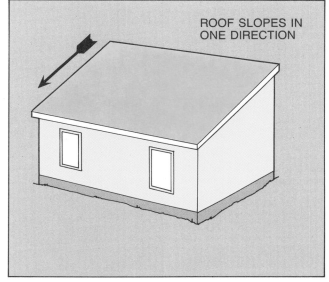

ROOF SLOPES IN ONE DIRECTION

FIGURE G-1. A shed-type roof has only one slope.

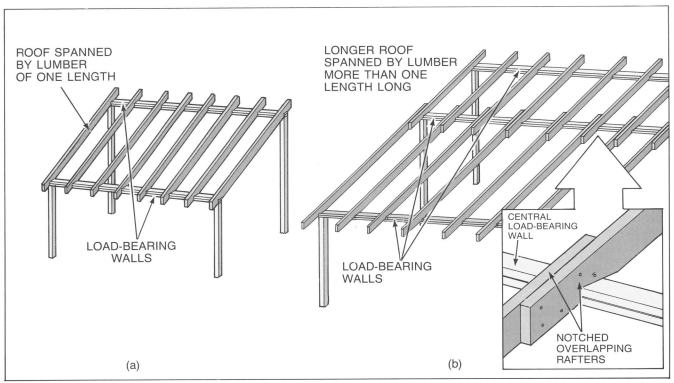

FIGURE G-2. (a) Most shed-type roofs are covered by lumber of one length. (b) Longer shed-type roofs must be spanned by lapped rafters over a load-bearing wall.

1. DETERMINING THE LENGTH OF A COMMON RAFTER FOR A SHED-TYPE ROOF

In determining the length of the rafters for a shed-type roof, there are several factors that are somewhat different from that of a gable roof.

First, the total rise is the *vertical* distance between the tops of the rafter plates on the two opposite walls (Figure G-1-1). The total run is figured by measuring the *horizontal* distance between the outside edges of the outside walls and subtracting the thickness of one wall (Figure G-1-1).

Second, you must allow for the overhang at both ends. Remember that the overhang on the upper side of the roof is measured from the *inside* edge of the rafter plate, whereas the overhang on the lower side is measured from the *outside* of the rafter plate to the trim (Figure G-1-1). Because of this difference in the way the overhangs are measured, the run of the lower and upper overhangs will *not* be the same.

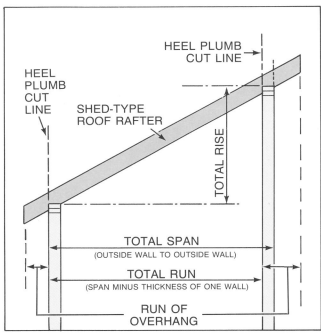

FIGURE G-1-1. The total run and total rise are computed differently from those of a gable roof.

Proceed as follows:

1. *Using the steps outlined in Section C-2, determine the length of the body of the rafter.*

    In your calculations, remember to take into account the exceptions noted earlier in this section.

2. *Add to your calculations the amount for the lower and upper overhangs.*

2. LAYING OUT A PATTERN SHED-TYPE RAFTER

Proceed as follows:

1. *Select a piece of lumber that is several inches longer than the calculated length needed.*

    The lumber needs to be 10″ to 12″ longer to allow for the angular cuts that will have to be made on the ends.

2. *Mark the heel plumb cut lines at both ends of the rafters (Figure G-2-1).*

    Remember to mark the crown edge. All rafters should be installed crown edge up.

3. *Using directions given earlier in this publication, mark the bird's mouths at both ends (Figure G-2-1).*

    There must be a bird's mouth at both ends since each end of the rafter will overlap a rafter plate.

4. *Mark for the overhangs, measuring from the heel plumb cut line at each end.*

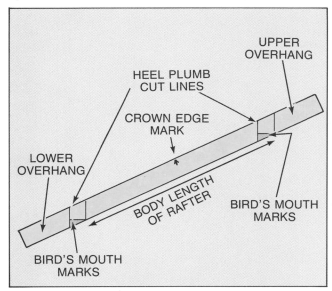

FIGURE G-2-1. Mark the heel plumb cut lines at either end of the shed-type rafter. Note that the body length is calculated from the front edge of the lower heel plumb cut line to the front edge of the upper heel plumb cut line.

As discussed earlier, the length of the overhang at the lower end will be shorter than the measured length at the upper end. The ends will be trimmed off evenly after the rafters are installed.

3. INSTALLING SHED-TYPE RAFTERS

A shed-type roof may be installed over an entire structure with an overhang on both ends, or it may be attached to a house as a roof over a porch or an addition to the structure. This latter installation will be discussed briefly at the end of this section.

This discussion assumes that the rafters are covering a structure with two load-bearing walls, one higher than the other to produce the angle (pitch) for which you cut a pattern rafter in the previous section.

Proceed as follows:

1. *Check the test rafter for fit.*

    This check should include placing the rafter on the marks made on the rafter plates on the upper and lower supporting walls, checking the bird's mouths for accuracy, and ensuring that the overhang portions of the rafter have been accurately laid out. The marking of the rafter plates should be made as discussed earlier in this publication.

2. *Cut the number of rafters needed, using the pattern rafter as a template.*

3. *Beginning from the corner of one end, place rafters on the marks made on the lower and upper rafter plates. Toenail the rafters in place with 16d nails. Toenail the lower end first, then the upper end (Figure G-3-1).*

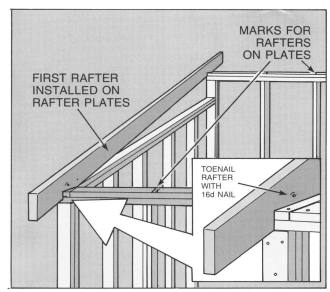

FIGURE G-3-1. Install rafters on marked rafter plates. Toenail the bottom, then the top, with 16d nails.

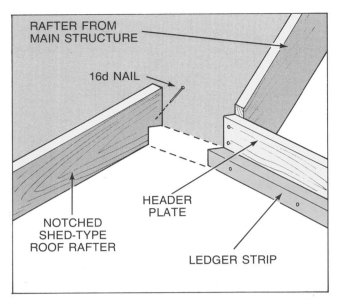

RAFTER FROM MAIN STRUCTURE

16d NAIL

HEADER PLATE

NOTCHED SHED-TYPE ROOF RAFTER

LEDGER STRIP

FIGURE G-3-2. When a shed-type roof is attached to another structure, a header must be fabricated and attached to the structure to secure the upper ends of the rafters. A ledger strip should be nailed to the header.

4. *Frame in the end walls, using the procedure outlined in Section D-2.*

If the shed-type roof is being attached to another structure, the procedure would be somewhat changed. A header is fabricated and attached to the structure (to the wall framing or the ends of the roof rafters) to which the roof is being attached. The rafters are then cut flush or notched to fit against the header at the top end (Figure G-3-2). A ledger strip should be nailed to the header to provide a surface for the notched shed-type roof rafters.

STUDY QUESTIONS

1. How many slopes does a shed-type roof have?

2. On what types of buildings are shed-type roofs most commonly found?

3. When a shed-type roof cannot be covered by a single length of lumber, where must the overlapped rafter ends be located?

4. On shed-type roofs, the total rise is the vertical distance between what two framing members?

5. Why are the runs of the lower and upper overhangs on a shed-type roof not equal?

6. In laying out a pattern rafter for a shed-type roof, why should the lumber selected be 10″ to 12″ longer than the calculated length needed?

7. To mark for the overhangs on a rafter for a shed-type roof, from which mark at each end do you measure?

8. When a shed-type roof covers the porch of a house, to what are the rafters attached at the top end?

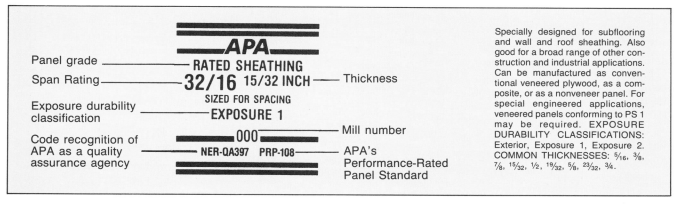

FIGURE H-1. A typical trademark you may find on plywood or other rated sheathing and an explanation of what the numbers and terms mean. For roof sheathing, the panel described in this example could be installed on supporting rafters spaced 32″ O.C.

American Plywood Association, *APA Design/Construction Guide, Residential & Commercial,* Page 6/7, September 1987.

Sheathing the roof is the last step in framing the roof assembly. There are several important functions of sheathing. It protects the framing beneath the sheathing, provides the foundation or base to which the finished roof material will be attached, and strengthens and stabilizes the entire roof assembly. The frame assembly appears to be very strong because it is constructed of larger material than many other areas of the house. In reality, it is very weak and unstable at this point.

Boards are still used by a few carpenters as sheathing and should be used for special applications (e.g., where wooden shingles or shakes will be used to cover the roof). However, the most widely used materials for sheathing today are panels made of plywood, oriented strand board, or some other composite board. These panels offer good strength to the roof assembly and are easily installed. For a more detailed discussion of plywood and other panel products, see *Floor Framing* (AAVIM, 1988).

Two numbers separated by a slash (e.g., 32/16) are seen on a typical panel trademark. These numbers are important; they denote the *span rating* (Figure H-1). The left-hand number (32) tells you that the maximum allowable spacing between supports when the material is used for *roof sheathing* is 32″ O.C. Supporting rafters on most roofs are spaced either 16″ or 24″ O.C. The number on the right side of the slash (16) denotes the maximum spacing between supports when the panel is used for *subflooring*. In both cases, the long dimension of the material must rest on three or more supports.

Estimating and installing roof sheathing is discussed under the following headings. The procedures outlined assume that panel material is being used for sheathing a gable roof.

1. Estimating Roof Sheathing
2. Installing Roof Sheathing

1. ESTIMATING ROOF SHEATHING

Panel sheathing materials can be expensive, so you want to buy only what you need. In order to make an intelligent estimate, you will need to make a *roof sheathing layout*.

Proceed as follows:

1. *Make a scaled sketch of the outside walls of the floor area of the house you are building (Figure H-1-1).*

   You may instead use the floor plans from your blueprints.

2. *Draw a line representing the ridge of the roof.*

   In our example, the ridge is located down the middle of the roof. It may help to label some of the things you've drawn to avoid confusion (Figure H-1-1).

3. *Draw a second set of lines (outside the lines representing the area covered by the house) to diagram the area of the roof (Figure H-1-1).*

This second set of lines should take into account the amount of overhang on the front and back sides, as well as at each end.

For accuracy, you will need to measure the length of a rafter from the ridgeboard to the trimmed eave edge on one side of the house. If the roof frame assembly is already in place, you may wish to take your measurements from an actual rafter and then measure the actual overall length of the roof. If you are working from scaled plans, take your measurements for the length of rafters from the side elevation of the house; take your measurements for the length of the roof from the front elevation.

NOTE: Because the rafters are installed at an angle, they must be measured by one of the methods described in order to ensure the accuracy of the scaled plan drawing that will be used to estimate the amount of sheathing required.

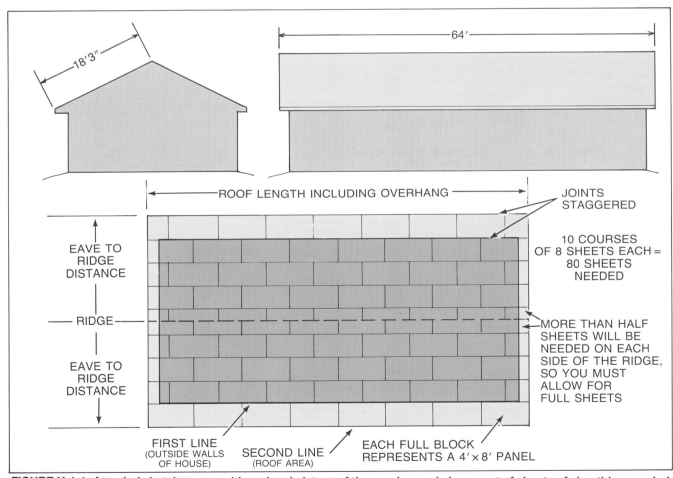

FIGURE H-1-1. A scaled sketch can provide a visual picture of the number and placement of sheets of sheathing needed for any particular roof. The elevation drawings at the top indicate the dimensions for the length and width of the roof area to be covered.

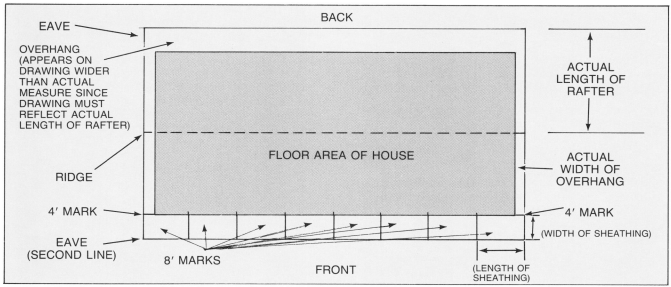

FIGURE H-1-2. Measure and draw lines on the scaled drawing representing the first run of 4′ × 8′ panels of sheathing.

4. *Starting from the second line representing the eave at the front of house, measure up 4′ (to scale) along the second line at the left (or right) side of the house (the line at right angles to the ridge) and mark that point. Repeat this procedure on the other side of the house. Draw a line connecting these two marks (Figure H-1-2).*

The 4′ marks represent the width of the first course (row) of full sheets of sheathing you will be drawing in your sketch.

5. *Starting from the left (or right) front corner of the house, divide the second line representing the front eave (the line along the axis of the ridge) into 8′ (to scale) segments. Starting from the same side of the house (left or right), divide the line between the 4′ marks into the same 8′ segments. Draw lines connecting each set of 8′ marks (Figure H-1-2).*

The 8′ marks represent the length of full sheets of sheathing. At this point, you have drawn the first course of roof sheathing.

6. *Working up from the first course of sheathing, measure and mark the second course using the same procedure as described in steps 4 and 5, **except** staggering the joints 4′ (Figure H-1-1).*

To create the stagger pattern, make your first block 4′ long (half the length of a full sheet).

7. *Continue to draw the courses of full and half sheets of sheathing until you get to the last course nearest the ridge.*

It is unlikely that this last course will be a full 4′ wide. If the area to be covered is 2′ wide or less, you may be able to use the other half of the sheet to continue the run of sheathing on the other side of the ridge. If the area is wider than 2′ (over half

of a 4′-wide sheet), you'll have to figure on using entire sheets of material, which could mean an excessive amount of waste.

8. *Continue to draw the courses of full and half sheets of sheathing on the other side of the ridge until you reach the eave line on the other side of the house.*

9. *Count the number of blocks representing full sheets of sheathing, and record the number.*

In the example, there are 75 full sheets needed. Because the courses on each side of the ridge are over 2′ wide, a full sheet will be needed on either side.

10. *Count the number of blocks representing half sheets of sheathing, and record the number.*

In the example, there are 10 half sheets (4′ × 4′) indicated.

11. *Divide the total number of half sheets by 2 to convert the number into full sheets.*

$$\frac{10}{2} = 5 \text{ full sheets}$$

NOTE: Round upward to the next full number if your answer leaves a fraction.

12. *Total your calculations from steps 10 and 11 to determine the number of sheets of sheathing needed to cover the roof surface.*

Using the example:

```
  75
+  5
────
  80   total number of 4′ × 8′ sheets
       of sheathing needed
```

NOTE: There is an alternate way to estimate the amount of sheathing required. To use this method, proceed as follows:

1. *To determine the number of sheets needed to span the length of the roof, divide the overall length of the roof frame by 8' (the length of a sheet of sheathing).*

   The length of the roof in the sample house is 64' (Figure H-1-1).

   $$\frac{64'}{8'} = 8 \text{ sheets}$$

2. *To determine the number of sheets needed to span the width of the roof, divide the rafter length by 4' (the width of a sheet of sheathing).*

   The length of a rafter for the sample house is 18'3" (Figure H-1-1). Since 3" is one-fourth (or .25) of a foot, this figure may be converted into 18.25'.

   $$\frac{18.25}{4} = 4.56 \text{ sheets}$$

3. *To determine the number of sheets needed for one side of a gable roof, multiply the results of steps 1 and 2.*

   $$\begin{array}{r} 4.56 \\ \times8 \\ \hline 36.48 \end{array} \text{ sheets for one side of roof}$$

4. *Multiply the total number of pieces needed for one side (36.48) by 2 (the number of sides to a gable roof).*

   $$\begin{array}{r} 36.48 \\ \times2 \\ \hline 72.96 \end{array} \text{ sheets for both sides of roof}$$

5. *Add 10% of the result from step 4 to the answer. Round your answer up or down to the nearest whole number.*

You can easily calculate 10% of any number by moving the decimal point one place to the left (or by multiplying by .10). Thus, 10% of 72.96 is 7.296. Rounded off, the answer is 7.

Adding these two figures together (72.96 + 7), you will determine the total number of sheets needed to sheath the sample house, with a 10% allowance for waste.

$$\begin{array}{r} 72.96 \\ +7.00 \\ \hline \end{array}$$
79.96, rounded to 80 total sheets needed

---

2. INSTALLING ROOF SHEATHING

After determining the number of sheets of sheathing needed, you are ready to install the panels on the rafter assembly, according to your scaled sketch.

Proceed as follows:

1. *Along the outside rafter on one side of the roof assembly, measure up 48" from the trim edge of the rafter or rough fascia, and mark that point (Figure H-2-1).*

2. *Repeat step 1 at the other end of the roof assembly.*

3. *Chalk a straight line from the 48" mark at one end of the roof assembly to the mark at the other end.*

4. *Mark the sheathing at the top and bottom edges every 16" or 24", depending on the rafter spacing (Figure H-2-2). Chalk lines across the sheathing connecting the marks at the top and bottom of the panels.*

   Begin this marking from the side edge of the rafter and sheathing (Figure H-2-2).

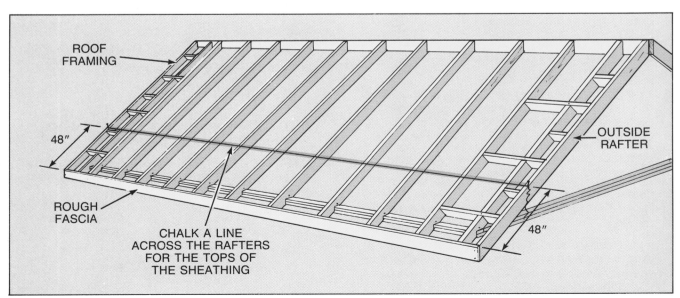

ROOF FRAMING

48"

ROUGH FASCIA

CHALK A LINE ACROSS THE RAFTERS FOR THE TOPS OF THE SHEATHING

OUTSIDE RAFTER

48"

FIGURE H-2-1. Measure up the rafters 48", and chalk a line as a guide to ensure the sheathing is properly aligned.

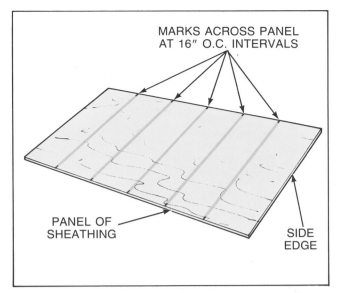

MARKS ACROSS PANEL
AT 16" O.C. INTERVALS

PANEL OF
SHEATHING

SIDE
EDGE

FIGURE H-2-2. Snap chalk lines across the sheathing using marks made along the edges at the same interval as the rafter spacing.

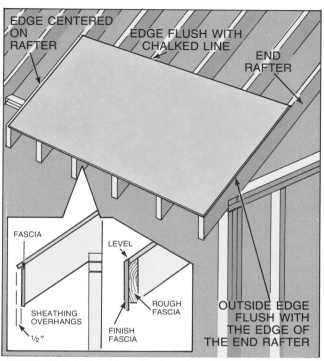

EDGE CENTERED ON RAFTER

EDGE FLUSH WITH CHALKED LINE

END RAFTER

FASCIA

LEVEL

ROUGH FASCIA

SHEATHING OVERHANGS

FINISH FASCIA

½"

OUTSIDE EDGE FLUSH WITH THE EDGE OF THE END RAFTER

FIGURE H-2-3. Position the first full sheet flush with the edge of the end rafter and the trimmed ends. The opposite edge should be centered on an intermediate rafter. The placement of the fascia (inset) may influence the positioning of the panels.

NOTE: The panels can be marked while tacked in place on the roof assembly; however, it is much easier and safer to measure and mark the panels before they are lifted up to the roof. The lines across the panels will be helpful as a guide when nailing takes place.

5. *Place the first sheet of 4' × 8' material at the lower right (or left) corner of the roof frame assembly on one side of the structure.*

The sheet should be positioned so that the outside edge is flush with the edge of the end rafter and so that the other end is centered on a rafter (Figure H-2-3). The top edge should be flush with the chalked line across the rafters. The way you plan to attach the fascia board to the ends of the rafters will determine whether the edge of the sheathing overhangs the tail of the rafters or is flush with the edge (Figure H-2-3).

6. *When the panel is in the correct position, attach it to the rafters with nails or staples from a pneumatic nailer, one nail (or staple) 1" from the edge of the sheathing on each of the marks made in step 4.*

Before nailing or stapling the panels, be sure that the rafters are properly aligned. At this point, the rafters are very flexible, and proper alignment is not difficult. Adjustments to the alignment will be impossible after the panels are nailed down securely. It is also *extremely* important that the first panel be positioned and attached squarely. These procedures should be done with great care and patience, since the first panel will determine the quality of the sheathing job.

Use 8d common nails spaced 6" O.C. on the edges and 10" O.C. on the intermediate rafters. If staples are used, they should be 1½" long and placed 4" O.C. on the edges and 8" O.C. on the intermediate rafters.

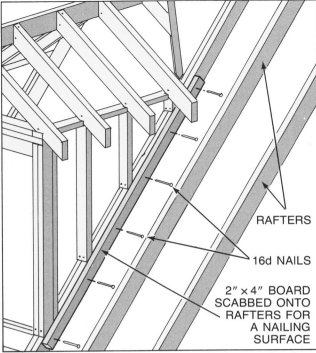

RAFTERS

16d NAILS

2" × 4" BOARD SCABBED ONTO RAFTERS FOR A NAILING SURFACE

FIGURE H-2-4. A strip may be attached to a rafter in an area where there is no nailing surface for sheathing. Nailing a strip to the rafter in this way is known as scabbing.

NOTE: All edges must be fastened down. Sometimes sheathing may butt against an obstacle, such as the side of a dormer, where there is no nailing surface. When this occurs, a 2" × 4" strip should be scabbed on (attached) to the side of a rafter to provide a nailing surface (Figure H-2-4).

7. *Complete the first course of plywood across the roof framework, making sure that each joint meets over an intermediate rafter. Repeat the procedures outlined in steps 4 and 6.*

8. *Place panel clips at the upper edge of each sheet between the rafters where the panels are not supported* (Figure H-2-5).

Panel clips (also called **H-clips**) are made of aluminum or steel and provide support in areas that would otherwise require blocking for support. They are made in sizes to accommodate ⅜", ½", ⅝", or ¾" panel thicknesses. They also create a small space between the upper and lower edges of adjoining panels that can prevent the bucking and warping of panels, which may be brought on by temperature and humidity changes.

NOTE: If panel clips are not used, a nail can be placed between the bottoms and tops of panels as a spacer.

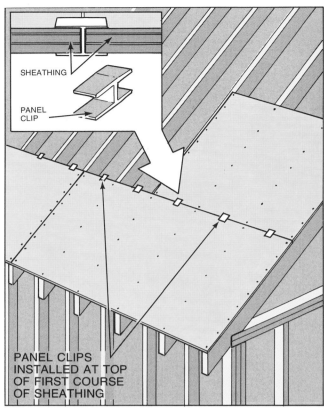

SHEATHING

PANEL CLIP

PANEL CLIPS INSTALLED AT TOP OF FIRST COURSE OF SHEATHING

FIGURE H-2-5. Steel or aluminum panel clips should be placed between the rafters at the tops of the lower panels.

9. *Start the second course with half a sheet of the panel material, marked as described in step 4. Fit the bottom edge into the panel clips on the top of the panel in the first course.*

The vertical seams of each course should be staggered from those in the preceding course, preferably by the width of half a panel (or 4') but no less than 32" from the nearest butt-joint. A **buttjoint** means that one piece of lumber (or panel) butts squarely against another.

10. *Nail the first panel in the second course as described in step 6.*

11. *Continue the second course using full sheets of the panel material, with a half sheet at the end. Install panel clips when you finish the course (at least one clip halfway between every other rafter).*

12. *Finish the side of the roof on which you are working by installing courses of panel sheets as described in steps 2–11.*

    NOTE: When you install the last course at the ridge, the panel will probably have to be trimmed to fit. The last panel on the first side to be sheathed should be trimmed flush with the rafters on the opposite side (Figure H-2-6). If you are installing a ridge vent, the sheathing should be trimmed so that it will be 1″ to 2″ short of the ridge to allow for ventilation.

13. *Sheath the opposite side of the roof frame as described in steps 1–12.*

    When you install the last course, trim the tops of the panels so that the material overlaps the edge of the panels from the other side (Figure H-2-6) or make allowance for the ridge vent.

14. *Trim off any overhang of sheathing at the ends of the fascia rafters so that it is flush with the edge.*

Safety is always a concern for those working on a roof frame. When you are working on a roof with a gentle slope, you should be able to work from the sheathing already put down as you progress toward the ridge.

When working on a steep roof, lengths of 2″ × 4″ boards should be laid across the sheathing at convenient intervals of 4′ to 6′ and temporarily attached to the rafters with 16d nails. These so-called **toeboards** will provide good footing for working on the roof and handholds in case of an emergency.

If there has been any sawing on the roof, be sure the area is swept clean before anyone attempts to walk on the assembly. Sawdust is very hazardous on a roof—even a roof with a low pitch.

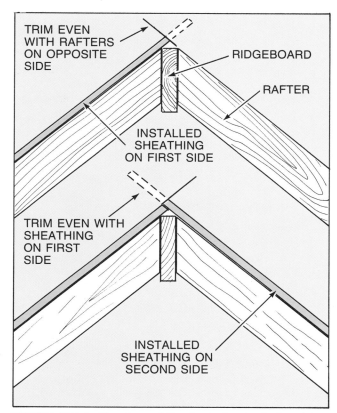

FIGURE H-2-6. The top of the last sheet of sheathing should be trimmed flush with the rafters on the other side of the ridgeboard. When the sheathing is installed on the other side, trim the edge flush with the sheathing on the first side.

85

STUDY QUESTIONS

1. Sheathing protects the roof framing and provides a base for attaching finished roof materials. What other major purpose does sheathing serve?

2. What is the most widely used sheathing material?

3. What are the dimensions (length and width) of typical sheathing?

4. If the trademark on sheathing material has two numbers separated by a slash, which number tells the span rating for roof sheathing?

5. **True or False**. In drawing a roof sheathing layout, the difference between the lines representing the outside walls and the lines representing the area of the roof is equal to the length of the overhang.

6. What is a course of sheathing?

7. The joints on sheathing should typically be staggered by how much?

8. If you estimate the amount of sheathing required using mathematical calculations rather than a roof sheathing layout, how much should be added to the result to allow for waste?

9. Why is sheathing marked every 16″ or 24″ at the top and bottom edges before it is installed?

10. What technique should you use to help you align the tops of sheathing material?

11. In installing sheathing, how far from the edge should nails be placed?

12. What term is used to describe the process of nailing a strip to a rafter to provide a nailing surface?

13. What devices are used to provide sheathing support between the rafters?

14. Why must a small space be left between the upper and lower edges of adjoining panels?

15. The sheathing at the top of the first side of the roof should be trimmed so that it is even with what roof component?

16. The sheathing at the top of the second side of the roof should be trimmed so that it is even with what roof component?

17. Toeboards provide good footing on a steep roof. At what intervals should they be placed?

18. How does sawdust affect roof safety?

Appendix

The following tables, which give the length of rafters for selected roof pitches from 3″ to 12″ rise per foot of run, were taken with permission from D.L. Sigmon, *A Framing Guide and Steel Square*, 5th edition, Cline-Sigmon Publishers, Box 367, Hickory, N.C. 28603, (704)322-5090.

Rafter Table for Rafters with 3″ Rise Per Foot of Run

Width of Building	Length of Main Rafters		Length of Hip/Valley Rafters		Rise of Roof	
Feet	Ft.	In.	Ft.	In.	Ft.	In.
2′	1′	0⅜″	1′	5¼″	0′	3″
3′	1′	6½″	2′	1⅞″	0′	4½″
4′	2′	0¾″	2′	10½″	0′	6″
5′	2′	6⅞″	3′	7⅛″	0′	7½″
6′	3′	1⅛″	4′	3¾″	0′	9″
7′	3′	7¼″	5′	0⅜″	0′	10½″
8′	4′	1½″	5′	8⅞″	1′	0″
9′	4′	7⅝″	6′	5½″	1′	1½″
10′	5′	1⅞″	7′	2⅛″	1′	3″
11′	5′	8″	7′	10¾″	1′	4½″
12′	6′	2¼″	8′	7⅜″	1′	6″
13′	6′	8⅜″	9′	4″	1′	7½″
14′	7′	2⅝″	10′	0⅝″	1′	9″
15′	7′	8¾″	10′	9¼″	1′	10½″
16′	8′	3″	11′	5⅞″	2′	0″
17′	8′	9⅛″	12′	2½″	2′	1½″
18′	9′	3⅜″	12′	11⅛″	2′	3″
19′	9′	9½″	13′	7¾″	2′	4½″
20′	10′	3¾″	14′	4⅜″	2′	6″
21′	10′	9⅞″	15′	1″	2′	7½″
22′	11′	4⅛″	15′	9⅝″	2′	9″
23′	11′	10¼″	16′	6¼″	2′	10½″
24′	12′	4⅜″	17′	2¾″	3′	0″
25′	12′	10⅝″	17′	11⅜″	3′	1½″
26′	13′	4¾″	18′	8″	3′	3″
27′	13′	11″	19′	4⅝″	3′	4½″
28′	14′	5⅛″	20′	1¼″	3′	6″
29′	14′	11⅜″	20′	9⅞″	3′	7½″
30′	15′	5½″	21′	6½″	3′	9″
31′	15′	11¾″	22′	3⅛″	3′	10½″
32′	16′	5⅞″	22′	11¾″	4′	0″
33′	17′	0⅛″	23′	8⅜″	4′	1½″
34′	17′	6¼″	24′	5″	4′	3″
35′	18′	0½″	25′	1⅝″	4′	4½″
36′	18′	6⅝″	25′	10¼″	4′	6″
37′	19′	0⅞″	26′	6⅞″	4′	7½″
38′	19′	7″	27′	3½″	4′	9″
39′	20′	1¼″	28′	0″	4′	10½″
40′	20′	7⅜″	28′	8⅝″	5′	0″
41′	21′	1⅝″	29′	5¼″	5′	1½″
42′	21′	7¾″	30′	1⅞″	5′	3″
43′	22′	2″	30′	10½″	5′	4½″
44′	22′	8⅛″	31′	7⅛″	5′	6″
45′	23′	2¼″	32′	3¾″	5′	7½″
46′	23′	8½″	33′	0⅜″	5′	9″
47′	24′	2⅝″	33′	9″	5′	10½″
48′	24′	8⅞″	34′	5⅝″	6′	0″

Length of shortest jack 16″ O.C. = 16½″
Length of shortest jack 24″ O.C. = 24¾″
Side cut for jacks, use 11⅝ and 12 cut on 12.
Side cut hip & valley, use 11⅞ and 12 cut on 12.

Rafter Table for Rafters with 4″ Rise Per Foot of Run

Width of Building	Length of Main Rafters		Length of Hip/Valley Rafters		Rise of Roof	
Feet	Ft.	In.	Ft.	In.	Ft.	In.
2′	1′	0⅝″	1′	5⅜″	0′	4″
3′	1′	7″	2′	2⅛″	0′	6″
4′	2′	1¼″	2′	10⅞″	0′	8″
5′	2′	7⅝″	3′	7⅝″	0′	10″
6′	3′	2″	4′	4½″	1′	0″
7′	3′	8¼″	5′	1″	1′	2″
8′	4′	2⅝″	5′	9¾″	1′	4″
9′	4′	8⅞″	6′	6½″	1′	6″
10′	5′	3¼″	7′	3⅛″	1′	8″
11′	5′	9⅝″	7′	11⅞″	1′	10″
12′	6′	3⅞″	8′	8⅝″	2′	0″
13′	6′	10¼″	9′	5⅜″	2′	2″
14′	7′	4½″	10′	2″	2′	4″
15′	7′	10⅞″	10′	10¾″	2′	6″
16′	8′	5¼″	11′	7½″	2′	8″
17′	8′	11½″	12′	4¼″	2′	10″
18′	9′	5⅞″	13′	0⅞″	3′	0″
19′	10′	0⅛″	13′	9⅝″	3′	2″
20′	10′	6½″	14′	6⅜″	3′	4″
21′	11′	0⅞″	15′	3⅛″	3′	6″
22′	11′	7⅛″	15′	11¾″	3′	8″
23′	12′	1½″	16′	8½″	3′	10″
24′	12′	7¾″	17′	5¼″	4′	0″
25′	13′	2⅛″	18′	2″	4′	2″
26′	13′	8½″	18′	10⅝″	4′	4″
27′	14′	2¾″	19′	7⅜″	4′	6″
28′	14′	9⅛″	20′	4⅛″	4′	8″
29′	15′	3⅜″	21′	0⅞″	4′	10″
30′	15′	9¾″	21′	9½″	5′	0″
31′	16′	4″	22′	6¼″	5′	2″
32′	16′	10⅜″	23′	3″	5′	4″
33′	17′	4¾″	23′	11¾″	5′	6″
34′	17′	11″	24′	8⅝″	5′	8″
35′	18′	5⅜″	25′	5⅛″	5′	10″
36′	18′	11⅝″	26′	1⅞″	6′	0″
37′	19′	6″	26′	10½″	6′	2″
38′	20′	0⅜″	27′	7¼″	6′	4″
39′	20′	6⅝″	28′	4″	6′	6″
40′	21′	1″	29′	0¾″	6′	8″
41′	21′	7¼″	29′	9⅜″	6′	10″
42′	22′	1⅝″	30′	6⅛″	7′	0″
43′	22′	8″	31′	2⅞″	7′	2″
44′	23′	2¼″	31′	11⅝″	7′	4″
45′	23′	8⅝″	32′	8¼″	7′	6″
46′	24′	2″	33′	5″	7′	8″
47′	24′	9¼″	34′	1¾″	7′	10″
48′	25′	3⅝″	34′	10½″	8′	0″

Length of shortest jack 16″ O.C. = 16⅞″.
Length of shortest jack 24″ O.C. = 25¼″
Side cut for jacks, use 11⅜ and 12 cut on 12.
Side cut hip & valley, use 11⅝ and 12 cut on 12.

Rafter Table for Rafters with 5″ Rise Per Foot of Run

Width of Building	Length of Main Rafters		Length of Hip/Valley Rafters		Rise of Roof	
Feet	Ft.	In.	Ft.	In.	Ft.	In.
2′	1′	1″	1′	5¾″	0′	5″
3′	1′	7½″	2′	2½″	0′	7½″
4′	2′	2″	2′	11⅜″	0′	10″
5′	2′	8½″	3′	8¼″	1′	0½″
6′	3′	3″	4′	5⅛″	1′	3″
7′	3′	9½″	5′	1⅞″	1′	5½″
8′	4′	4″	5′	10¾″	1′	8″
9′	4′	10½″	6′	7⅝″	1′	10½″
10′	5′	5″	7′	4½″	2′	1″
11′	5′	11½″	8′	1¼″	2′	3½″
12′	6′	6″	8′	10⅛″	2′	6″
13′	7′	0½″	9′	7″	2′	8½″
14′	7′	7″	10′	3⅞″	2′	11″
15′	8′	1½″	11′	0¾″	3′	1½″
16′	8′	8″	11′	9½″	3′	4″
17′	9′	2½″	12′	6⅜″	3′	6½″
18′	9′	9″	13′	3¼″	3′	9″
19′	10′	3½″	14′	0⅛″	3′	11½″
20′	10′	10″	14′	8⅞″	4′	2″
21′	11′	4½″	15′	5¾″	4′	4½″
22′	11′	11″	16′	2⅝″	4′	7″
23′	12′	5½″	16′	11½″	4′	9½″
24′	13′	0″	17′	8¼″	5′	0″
25′	13′	6½″	18′	5⅛″	5′	2½″
26′	14′	1″	19′	2″	5′	5″
27′	14′	7½″	19′	10⅞″	5′	7½″
28′	15′	2″	20′	7⅝″	5′	10″
29′	15′	8½″	21′	4½″	6′	0½″
30′	16′	3″	22′	1⅜″	6′	3″
31′	16′	9½″	22′	10¼″	6′	5½″
32′	17′	4″	23′	7⅛″	6′	8″
33′	17′	10½″	24′	3⅞″	6′	10½″
34′	18′	5″	25′	0¾″	7′	1″
35′	18′	11½″	25′	9⅝″	7′	3½″
36′	19′	6″	26′	6½″	7′	6″
37′	20′	0½″	27′	3¼″	7′	8½″
38′	20′	7″	28′	0⅛″	7′	11″
39′	21′	1½″	28′	9″	8′	1½″
40′	21′	8″	29′	5⅞″	8′	4″
41′	22′	2½″	30′	2⅝″	8′	6½″
42′	22′	9″	30′	11½″	8′	9″
43′	23′	3½″	31′	8⅜″	8′	11½″
44′	23′	10″	32′	5¼″	9′	2″
45′	24′	4½″	33′	2⅛″	9′	4½″
46′	24′	11″	33′	10⅞″	9′	7″
47′	25′	5½″	34′	7¾″	9′	9½″
48′	26′	0″	35′	4⅝″	10′	0″

Length of shortest jack 16″ O.C. = 17⅜″.
Length of shortest jack 24″ O.C. = 26″.
Side cut for jacks, use 11⅛ and 12 cut on 12.
Side cut hip & valley, use 11½ and 12 cut on 12.

Rafter Table for Rafters with 6″ Rise Per Foot of Run

Width of Building	Length of Main Rafters		Length of Hip/Valley Rafters		Rise of Roof	
Feet	Ft.	In.	Ft.	In.	Ft.	In.
2′	1′	1⅜″	1′	6″	0′	6″
3′	1′	8⅛″	2′	3″	0′	9″
4′	2′	2⅞″	3′	0″	1′	0″
5′	2′	9½″	3′	9″	1′	3″
6′	3′	4¼″	4′	6″	1′	6″
7′	3′	11″	5′	3″	1′	9″
8′	4′	5⅝″	6′	0″	2′	0″
9′	5′	0⅜″	6′	9″	2′	3″
10′	5′	7⅛″	7′	6″	2′	6″
11′	6′	1¾″	8′	3″	2′	9″
12′	6′	8½″	9′	0″	3′	0″
13′	7′	3¼″	9′	9″	3′	3″
14′	7′	9⅞″	10′	6″	3′	6″
15′	8′	4⅝″	11′	3″	3′	9″
16′	8′	11⅜″	12′	0″	4′	0″
17′	9′	6″	12′	9″	4′	3″
18′	10′	0¾″	13′	6″	4′	6″
19′	10′	7½″	14′	3″	4′	9″
20′	11′	2⅛″	15′	0″	5′	0″
21′	11′	8⅞″	15′	9″	5′	3″
22′	12′	3⅝″	16′	6″	5′	6″
23′	12′	10¼″	17′	3″	5′	9″
24′	13′	5″	18′	0″	6′	0″
25′	13′	11¾″	18′	9″	6′	3″
26′	14′	6⅜″	19′	6″	6′	6″
27′	15′	1⅛″	20′	3″	6′	9″
28′	15′	7⅞″	21′	0″	7′	0″
29′	16′	2½″	21′	9″	7′	3″
30′	16′	9¼″	22′	6″	7′	6″
31′	17′	4″	23′	3″	7′	9″
32′	17′	10⅝″	24′	0″	8′	0″
33′	18′	5⅜″	24′	9″	8′	3″
34′	19′	0⅛″	25′	6″	8′	6″
35′	19′	6¾″	26′	3″	8′	9″
36′	20′	1½″	27′	0″	9′	0″
37′	20′	8¼″	27′	9″	9′	3″
38′	21′	2⅞″	28′	6″	9′	6″
39′	21′	9⅝″	29′	3″	9′	9″
40′	22′	4⅜″	30′	0″	10′	0″
41′	22′	11″	30′	9″	10′	3″
42′	23′	5¾″	31′	6″	10′	6″
43′	24′	0½″	32′	3″	10′	9″
44′	24′	7⅛″	33′	0″	11′	0″
45′	25′	1⅞″	33′	9″	11′	3″
46′	25′	8⅝″	34′	6″	11′	6″
47′	26′	3¼″	35′	3″	11′	9″
48′	26′	10″	36′	0″	12′	0″

Length of shortest jack 16″ O.C. = 17⅞″.
Length of shortest jack 24″ O.C. = 26⅞″.
Side cut for jacks, use 10¾ and 12 cut on 12.
Side cut hip & valley, use 11¼ and 12 cut on 12.

Rafter Table for Rafters with 7″ Rise Per Foot of Run

Width of Building	Length of Main Rafters		Length of Hip/Valley Rafters		Rise of Roof	
Feet	Ft.	In.	Ft.	In.	Ft.	In.
2′	1′	1⅞″	1′	6⅜″	0′	7″
3′	1′	8⅞″	2′	3½″	0′	10½″
4′	2′	3¾″	3′	0¾″	1′	2″
5′	2′	10¾″	3′	9⅞″	1′	5½″
6′	3′	5⅝″	4′	7⅛″	1′	9″
7′	4′	0⅝″	5′	4¼″	2′	0½″
8′	4′	7⅝″	6′	1⅜″	2′	4″
9′	5′	2½″	6′	10⅝″	2′	7½″
10′	5′	9½″	7′	7¾″	2′	11″
11′	6′	4⅜″	8′	5″	3′	2½″
12′	6′	11⅜″	9′	2⅛″	3′	6″
13′	7′	6¼″	9′	11⅜″	3′	9½″
14′	8′	1¼″	10′	8½″	4′	1″
15′	8′	8¼″	11′	5⅝″	4′	4½″
16′	9′	3⅛″	12′	2⅞″	4′	8″
17′	9′	10⅛″	13′	0″	4′	11½″
18′	10′	5″	13′	9¼″	5′	3″
19′	11′	0″	14′	6⅜″	5′	6½″
20′	11′	6⅞″	15′	3⅝″	5′	10″
21′	12′	1⅞″	16′	0¾″	6′	1½″
22′	12′	8⅞″	16′	9⅞″	6′	5″
23′	13′	3¾″	17′	7⅛″	6′	8½″
24′	13′	10¾″	18′	4¼″	7′	0″
25′	14′	5⅝″	19′	1½″	7′	3½″
26′	15′	0⅝″	19′	10⅝″	7′	7″
27′	15′	7½″	20′	7⅞″	7′	10½″
28′	16′	2½″	21′	5″	8′	2″
29′	16′	9⅜″	22′	2⅛″	8′	5½″
30′	17′	4⅜″	22′	11⅜″	8′	9″
31′	17′	11¼″	23′	8½″	9′	0½″
32′	18′	6¼″	24′	5¾″	9′	4″
33′	19′	1¼″	25′	2⅞″	9′	7½″
34′	19′	8⅛″	26′	0⅛″	9′	11″
35′	20′	3⅛″	26′	9¼″	10′	2½″
36′	20′	10″	27′	6⅜″	10′	6″
37′	21′	5″	28′	3⅝″	10′	9½″
38′	22′	0″	29′	0¾″	11′	1″
39′	22′	6⅞″	29′	10″	11′	4½″
40′	23′	1⅞″	30′	7⅛″	11′	8″
41′	23′	8¾″	31′	4⅜″	11′	11½″
42′	24′	3¾″	32′	1½″	12′	3″
43′	24′	10⅝″	32′	10⅝″	12′	6½″
44′	25′	5⅝″	33′	7⅞″	12′	10″
45′	26′	0⅝″	34′	5″	13′	1½″
46′	26′	7½″	35′	2¼″	13′	5″
47′	27′	2½″	35′	11⅜″	13′	8½″
48′	27′	9⅜″	36′	8⅝″	14′	0″

Length of shortest jack 16″ O.C. = 18½″.
Length of shortest jack 24″ O.C. = 27¾″.
Side cut for jacks, use 10⅜ and 12 cut on 12.
Side cut hip & valley, use 11⅛ and 12 cut on 12.

Rafter Table for Rafters with 8″ Rise Per Foot of Run

Width of Building	Length of Main Rafters		Length of Hip/Valley Rafters		Rise of Roof	
Feet	Ft.	In.	Ft.	In.	Ft.	In.
2′	1′	2⅜″	1′	6¾″	0′	8″
3′	1′	9⅝″	2′	4⅛″	1′	0″
4′	2′	4⅞″	3′	1½″	1′	4″
5′	3′	0″	3′	10⅞″	1′	8″
6′	3′	7¼″	4′	8¼″	2′	0″
7′	4′	2½″	5′	5⅝″	2′	4″
8′	4′	9¾″	6′	3″	2′	8″
9′	5′	4⅞″	7′	0⅜″	3′	0″
10′	6′	0⅛″	7′	9¾″	3′	4″
11′	6′	7⅜″	8′	7¼″	3′	8″
12′	7′	2½″	9′	4⅝″	4′	0″
13′	7′	9¾″	10′	2″	4′	4″
14′	8′	5″	10′	11⅜″	4′	8″
15′	9′	0⅛″	11′	8¾″	5′	0″
16′	9′	7⅜″	12′	6⅛″	5′	4″
17′	10′	2⅝″	13′	3½″	5′	8″
18′	10′	9¾″	14′	0⅞″	6′	0″
19′	11′	5″	14′	10¼″	6′	4″
20′	12′	0¼″	15′	7⅝″	6′	8″
21′	12′	7½″	16′	5″	7′	0″
22′	13′	2⅝″	17′	2⅜″	7′	4″
23′	13′	9⅞″	17′	11¾″	7′	8″
24′	14′	5⅛″	18′	9⅛″	8′	0″
25′	15′	0¼″	19′	6½″	8′	4″
26′	15′	7½″	20′	3⅞″	8′	8″
27′	16′	2¾″	21′	1¼″	9′	0″
28′	16′	9⅞″	21′	10⅝″	9′	4″
29′	17′	5⅛″	22′	8″	9′	8″
30′	18′	0⅜″	23′	5⅜″	10′	0″
31′	18′	7½″	24′	2¾″	10′	4″
32′	19′	2¾″	25′	0⅛″	10′	8″
33′	19′	10″	25′	9⅝″	11′	0″
34′	20′	5⅛″	26′	7″	11′	4″
35′	21′	0⅜″	27′	4⅜″	11′	8″
36′	21′	7⅝″	28′	1¾″	12′	0″
37′	22′	2¾″	28′	11⅛″	12′	4″
38′	22′	10″	29′	8½″	12′	8″
39′	23′	5¼″	30′	5⅞″	13′	0″
40′	24′	0½″	31′	3¼″	13′	4″
41′	24′	7⅝″	32′	0⅝″	13′	8″
42′	25′	2⅞″	32′	10″	14′	0″
43′	25′	10⅛″	33′	7⅜″	14′	4″
44′	26′	5¼″	34′	4¾″	14′	8″
45′	27′	0½″	35′	2⅛″	15′	0″
46′	27′	7¾″	35′	11½″	15′	4″
47′	28′	2⅞″	36′	8⅞″	15′	8″
48′	28′	10⅛″	37′	6¼″	16′	0″

Length of shortest jack 16″ O.C. = 19¼″.
Length of shortest jack 24″ O.C. = 28⅞″.
Side cut for jacks, use 10 and 12 cut on 12.
Side cut hip & valley, use 10⅞ and 12 cut on 12.

Rafter Table for Rafters
with 12″ Rise Per Foot of Run

Width of Building	Length of Main Rafters		Length of Hip/Valley Rafters		Rise of Roof	
Feet	Ft.	In.	Ft.	In.	Ft.	In.
2′	1′	5″	1′	8¾″	1′	0″
3′	2′	1½″	2′	7⅛″	1′	6″
4′	2′	10″	3′	5⅝″	2′	0″
5′	3′	6⅜″	4′	4″	2′	6″
6′	4′	2⅞″	5′	2⅜″	3′	0″
7′	4′	11⅜″	6′	0¾″	3′	6″
8′	5′	7⅞″	6′	11⅛″	4′	0″
9′	6′	4⅜″	7′	9½″	4′	6″
10′	7′	0⅞″	8′	7⅞″	5′	0″
11′	7′	9⅜″	9′	6⅜″	5′	6″
12′	8′	5⅞″	10′	4⅝″	6′	0″
13′	9′	2¼″	11′	3⅛″	6′	6″
14′	9′	10¾″	12′	1½″	7′	0″
15′	10′	7¼″	12′	11⅞″	7′	6″
16′	11′	3¾″	13′	10¼″	8′	0″
17′	12′	0¼″	14′	8⅝″	8′	6″
18′	12′	8¾″	15′	7″	9′	0″
19′	13′	5¼″	16′	5½″	9′	6″
20′	14′	1¾″	17′	3¾″	10′	0″
21′	14′	10⅛″	18′	2¼″	10′	6″
22′	15′	6⅝″	19′	0⅝″	11′	0″
23′	16′	3⅛″	19′	11″	11′	6″
24′	16′	11⅝″	20′	9⅜″	12′	0″
25′	17′	8⅛″	21′	7¾″	12′	6″
26′	18′	4⅝″	22′	6¼″	13′	0″
27′	19′	1⅛″	23′	4⅝″	13′	6″
28′	19′	9⅝″	24′	3″	14′	0″
29′	20′	6⅛″	25′	1⅜″	14′	6″
30′	21′	2½″	25′	11¾″	15′	0″
31′	21′	11″	26′	10⅛″	15′	6″
32′	22′	7½″	27′	8½″	16′	0″
33′	23′	4″	28′	6⅞″	16′	6″
34′	24′	0½″	29′	5⅜″	17′	0″
35′	24′	9″	30′	3¾″	17′	6″
36′	25′	5½″	31′	2⅛″	18′	0″
37′	26′	2″	32′	0½″	18′	6″
38′	26′	10⅜″	32′	10⅞″	19′	0″
39′	27′	6⅞″	33′	9¼″	19′	6″
40′	28′	3⅜″	34′	7⅝″	20′	0″
41′	28′	11⅞″	35′	6⅛″	20′	6″
42′	29′	8⅜″	36′	4½″	21′	0″
43′	30′	4⅞″	37′	2⅞″	21′	6″
44′	31′	1⅜″	38′	1¼″	22′	0″
45′	31′	9⅞″	38′	11⅝″	22′	6″
46′	32′	6¼″	39′	10″	23′	0″
47′	33′	2¾″	40′	8⅜″	23′	6″
48′	33′	11¼″	41′	6⅞″	24′	0″

Length of shortest jack 16″ O.C. = 22⅝″.
Length of shortest jack 24″ O.C. = 33⅞″.
Side cut for jacks, use 8½ and 12 cut on 12.
Side cut hip & valley, use 9⅞ and 12 cut on 12.

Index

BILL OF MATERIALS

Pg No_____

Project:_____ Date_____

ITEM NAME	NUMBER NEEDED	DIMENSION OR SIZE	BOARD FEET	PRICE PER UNIT	ESTIMATED COST		SPECIFICATIONS AND OTHER COMMENTS

Total this sheet $_____

Additional information

94

CONTRIBUTORS OF LITERATURE AND OTHER MATERIALS USED IN THIS PUBLICATION

Companies and Institutions

American Lumber Standards Committee, P.O. Box 210, Germantown, Maryland 20874

Georgia-Pacific Corporation, 133 Peachtree Street, N.E., Atlanta, Georgia 30348

Sigmon, D.L., A Framing Guide and Steel Square, Revised edition, Cline-Sigmon Publishers, Box 367, Hickory, N.C. 28603

Southern Building Code Congress, 900 Montclair Road, Birmingham, Alabama 35213

Southern Forest Products Association, P.O. Box 52468, New Orleans, Louisiana 70152

Southeastern Lumber Manufacturers Association, P.O. Box 1788, Forest Park, Georgia 30061

Southern Pine Inspection Bureau, 4709 Scenic Highway, Pensacola, Florida 32504

Western Wood Products Association, Yeon Building, 522 S.W. Fifth Avenue, Portland, Oregon 97204

Other Contributors

John Q. West and Clanton Black, Dearing Development Corporation, Athens, GA

Roy Turk and Von Jackson, Turk Construction Company, Athens, GA

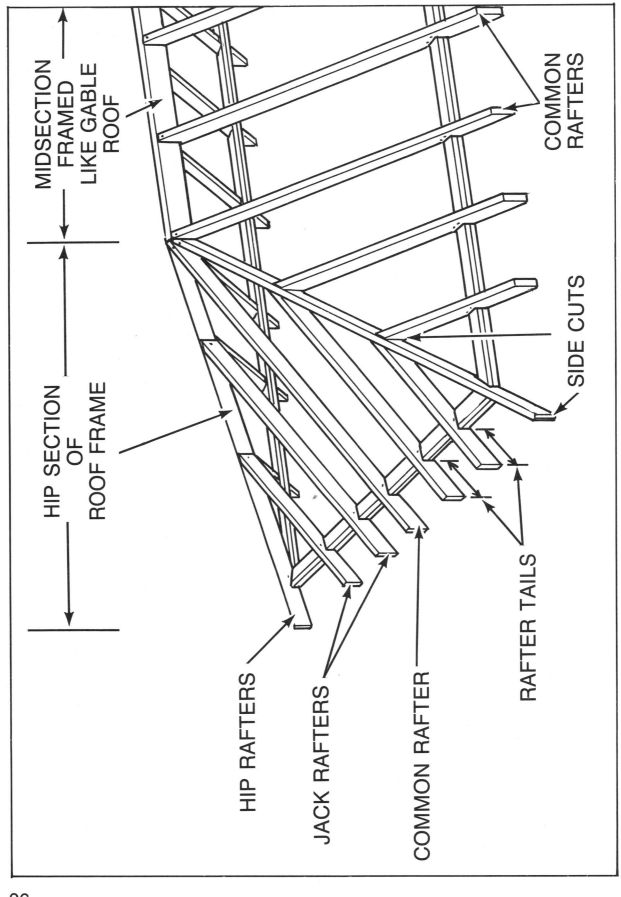

MIDSECTION FRAMED LIKE GABLE ROOF

HIP SECTION OF ROOF FRAME

COMMON RAFTERS

SIDE CUTS

HIP RAFTERS

JACK RAFTERS

COMMON RAFTER

RAFTER TAILS

The ends of a hip roof assembly are constructed of unique components that are figured, cut, and installed differently from the central section.